ACTION/ITEMS

The Collected Plays of
Tony Abatemarco
VOLUME I

Book jacket design: Dean Abatemarco
Cover photo: James Fawcett
Biographical Etching: Dan McCleary
Type formatting: Juno Pinder

First Edition
ISBN 97809 99869529

First published in the United States in 2018 by
f-stop Books

Contents

ACTION FOREWORD *by Michael Kearns*

I have always been somewhat intimidated by Tony Abatemarco. Throughout the eighties, our paths ineluctably crossed because we were both headliners on the equity waiver circuit in Los Angeles even though Tony's resume was gaining traction by accumulating heady material while I seemed to be trailing behind because of my sexually-charged choices. At one point, we had shows running in the same theater; consider the titles: Tony was one of the writers of *Brain Hotel*, I was in *The International Stud.*

However, as the years unraveled, it became evident that our similarities were far greater than our differences. Abatemarco possesses an artistic mission that incorporates sexuality with intellect, entertaining audiences that extend beyond the boundaries of the theater we shared (of less than 99 seats) while addressing urgent issues that affect humanity without borders.

Taken as a whole, the four theater works that comprise *ACTION ITEMS, Part I of The Collected Plays of Tony Abatemarco* could unwittingly be perceived as an autobiography. At one of our recent personal/professional lunch confabs, Abatemarco acknowledged, "All writing is autobiographical." Look closely and you'll find Abatemarco's blood, sweat, and tears saturating every page, resulting in a form of artistry that simultaneously illuminates the human condition through the constructs of imaginative storytelling, borne from real-life characters and situations, while never losing sight of the larger picture.

The first two—*Four Fathers* and *Cologne*, written in the twentieth century, depicting two distinct periods of time—are theatrical memoirs, a specific genre heavily cultivated by the actor-writers among us. While this artist of multiple disciplines had already tried on his writerly chapeau, it was the death of his father that compelled him, and perhaps freed him, to begin to write for the stage, a terrain as comfortable to Abatemarco as soil is to most of us. To "eulogize," as he so aptly describes his rich work, yes, but that is only a component of his work's influence which contains unknown quanta of tonic to heal misfirings of the heart.

In the overcrowded world of solo performance, Abatemarco immediately established himself as an anomaly because of his exquisite command of language. The success of most one-person pieces relies heavily on the melding of the artist's skills as performer-slash-writer. In many (if not most) instances, the soloist's performative skills might even trick the audience into thinking the writing is stronger than it is.

Not so with Abatemarco, who had proven himself as a masterful actor, of supple voice and body, having secured a solid theater resume and an enviable IMDB page before he uttered the first lines of *Four Fathers*. Also in contrast to many (if not most) of his peers who were going solo, this was not the studied career move of a fledgling who expected to be catapulted into a new stratosphere of Hollywood's elite; in truth, Abatemarco's brazen honesty has been known to derail rather than beguile.

By all accounts, one needn't even imagine the performances he delivered on the stage in *Four Fathers* or *Cologne* to be certain that on the page, Abatemarco has written literature.

Incorporating a bit of Greek mythology and references to Shakespeare, *Four Fathers* takes us on a journey into the psyche of the man Abatemarco believes his father to be, a flesh and blood hero, but a hero nonetheless. The writing is theatrical but the purple ink is delicately applied and the writing is always accessible; it pulls us into the story with muscle. Stark on the page in contrast to the flowing prose, *Four Fathers* features chants and raps, creating rhythms and cadences that poetically heighten emotionality for the reader or the live audience.

"Am I dying to honor my Father, or am I living to better him?" the Narrator asks, a question that drives the action of this fraught father-son relationship. Death is pervasive. A year after our Narrator's mother dies, he spends time with his Dad in their Lincoln Continental and the descriptions that Abatemarco conjures, with elegant specificity, intensify the bond with his father while embellishing his family portrait with reminiscences that exalt the female durability of their roots. Of his grandma, he says, "In her satin nightgown and clouds of lilac powder, she'd envelop me with ample pats and kisses."

Abatemarco's first entry moves through adolescence (a peek of what's to come in *Cologne*) and the ineluctable separation from Dad: "So I set out to conquer a world that he'd ignored. A world of letters. Speeches. Academia. I pinned things to my shirtfront that he could never own. Eloquence. Psychology. Man-love."

And playwriting, deftly proven in the final moments of *Four Fathers* when Abatemarco weaves the myth of Daedalus and his son Icarus, who create wings from the wax of candles in order to take flight from the tower where they are imprisoned, into his personal narrative. Abatemarco and his father (or perhaps his four fathers) begin a breathtaking, magical flight into the sun as the music swells and the lights fade to black.

But not before he reveals to his Dad, "I told you about the man I love, and you said, 'I still love you.'"

To love a man is the action item that catapults *Cologne*, a piece of literature that can also be labeled a theatrical memoir, especially considering how it rivets on a narrow period of time and swirls around one shocking event. Written in the third person but decidedly in the playwright's fervid voice, *Cologne* is a morality tale for all seasons but especially cogent for those of us who have struggled with the inequities that misconstrue our identities.

As many of these boys-will-be-be-boys tales do, this *roman à clef* starts innocently enough: rowdy boys in a swimming pool where the oldest of the tribe, 18-year-old Bobby, proves his prowess by sticking his dick in the pool's vacuum hose, simulating a blow job. Billy is Bobby's 16-year-old brother and the best friend of 14-year-old Tony. "Sex was all that mattered to them," we are warned.

With "a Marlon Brando slouch and five o'clock shadow," Tony found sex, often "in some strange man's car" while alternately trying to fit in at school by serial-dating too many girls. When he lures Bobby into a sexual assignation, Abatemarco describes the clumsiness of the encounter while capturing the erotic pain of conflicted adolescent emotionality.

Bobby joins the Marines but while home for the holidays, Tony, luxuriating in "a delicious melancholia," invites him over to celebrate New Year's Eve, taking advantage of a house full of booze but empty of family. The twosome essentially repeats the same dance from the previous summer but this time in a bed, naked. We learn that "Tony smells too sweet and Bobby too musky."

For anyone who has even paid scant attention to the evolution of the gay community's struggle, what happens next may be familiar territory but the scenes do not play out predictably in Abatemarco's mercurial hands. *Cologne's* plot swerves dangerously; after Tony is "arbitrarily jumped and beaten unconscious by a local gang," he aligns himself with a group of "losers and fuck-ups mostly."

The Oppressed becomes the Oppressor, a trope that extends beyond the world of gay men but Abatemarco's deep empathy for himself and his tribe reveals unflinching insights into the way—how many years after *The Boys In The Band*?—we still "hate ourselves so much."

When the "fearless troublemakers" discover a stack of pornographic chap-books, two of them bursting with homo content, Tony uses the prickly situation to render himself homo-free by intimating the porn belongs to Bobby. Tony complies when the gang forces him to procure Bobby—and then?—"just what Tony didn't want to happen was happening."

Smells suffuse Abatemarco's storyline, wafting from his characters' bodies to provide clues to their interior lives; the personas they wish to aromatically project, that is. But these boy-men are also awash in other sensorial memories that surely haunt: the sounds grunts, kicks, thuds and the litany of poisonous names Bobby is called that I will refrain from "repeating" here because the words hurt too much.

"Sticks and stones may break my bones but words may never hurt me" is a fake homily that Abatemarco doesn't have to reference but the singsong saying propels the remaining pages of *Cologne*. (Listen carefully—or should I say, read carefully?—and you'll realize that the hurt of those words largely propels the action of the remainder of the book.)

There is a final encounter with Bobby in which language is stuffed deep inside, percolating under the scene's framework; here, Abatemarco's absence of words is proof of his incandescent writing.

Tony (the character, not the playwright) needn't perform an aria of remorse or a sermon of self-awareness: the hallmarks of bad solo pieces. He moves on.

He finds himself in a bar in Boston on the weekend of the Stonewall demonstration (1969) that would alter the course of GLBTQ history: "A thousand different aftershaves billowed up through the scent of cigarettes and pot and perspiration. English Leather, Royal Lime, Old Spice, Mennen Skin Bracer, Aramis, Bay Rum, Brut, Aqua Velva. So this was it, the mythical land of anything goes." The metaphorical mélange of fragrances is as political as it is personal.

After the "End of Play" instruction, the playwright dedicates his work and apologizes to Matthew Shephard and "the several thousand victims of hate crimes every year." Abatemarco's candor is breathtaking but we knew this already, didn't we? Not because of an apoplectic apology delivered by the character at full throttle but rather by the "truth" of the writer's "fictitious" story.

The second half of Abatemarco's equally heartwarming and heart-wrenching items are two multi-character plays, signifying a leap for the playwright into the twenty-first century, representing a personal maturity on the page that contrasts with the realities of uncertainty that grips America as *ACTION ITEMS* goes to press. The action items of Abatemarco's title, especially those addressed in *Forever House* but unquestionably built upon in *Beautified*, will consume Americans for years, if not decades, to come.

During the decade-plus that separate the scents of men's fragrances that permeate *Cologne* and the scenes of *Beautified* that are melded by hairspray, Abatemarco and I officially partner on numerous artistic projects, focusing much of our energy on the Skylight Theatre Company where politics have moved from a supporting to a leading role in how we envision our brand. The intellect (his) and sexuality (mine) of decades prior have morphed and merged.

Beautified and *Forever House* were written in the glow of the Obama presidency. Both plays decidedly reflect the hope that Barack and Michelle had instilled in us; it's as if they are unseen characters in Abatemarco's plays, powerful offstage influences—guardian angels, maybe?—reminding us that even in the midst of our conflicts and strife, we were safe. Our rights—as women who need to get abortions, as some members of the GLBTQ community who want to get married and have children—these unalienable rights were protected.

In their published form, likely to inspire live productions, the two plays became virtual "period pieces" overnight, thanks to deliberate steps of this administration to move backwards and trounce on what had become the playwright's given circumstances. They must be played, if you'll pardon the expression, straight.

There is a significant chasm on the political landscape that will intellectually point to Abatemarco's work as either a blissful flashback or a demonic transgression but render it potentially more powerful than ever.

Candy, the leading lady of *Beautified*, is a piece of work; her contradictions contain contradictions, resulting in an assortment of traits that don't immediately please all palates but Abatemarco applies his palette of skills and employs direct address to the audience, delivered by Candy: "I have an aversion to maudlin claptrap with gooey centers," she teases, engaging in a bit of silly wordplay (kinda like what I'm doing now). Before the play begins, she also informs us that it is 1969. (She doesn't tell us that *Cologne* ended the same year.)

In the first encounter of many that she will have with Mike, the hairdresser extraordinaire who becomes her Everything, she also reveals that she is a Republican and getting an abortion at a "unmarked storefront around the corner" from the salon.

Candy's Republicanism is a blood red thread that plays throughout *Beautified*, often as a comedic device. However, her partisanship may land differently on audiences in 2018 than it did when the play premiered in 2012. A larger challenge lies with how a post-Trump audience might respond to Mike's secretive confession to Candy in the play's early exchanges when, referring to his homosexuality, he whispers: "I was sick."

As painful as it may be to digest, so many of the extreme biases that we assumed had been eradicated from the "books" and from the consciousness of America's conscience are making a draconian comeback since Abatemarco's twenty-first century offerings were first produced. Gay men and their supporters (including most people on the left and more than are often acknowledged on the right) might react differently upon hearing a gay man say that he had accepted the "sick" label.

Abatemarco is eulogizing again, not even bothering to change the name of the older brother, sixteen years his senior, whose gay navigations were driven by fear, a fear that Abatemarco doesn't avoid detailing. "It's a mental illness," his brother (the character) says. For the record, this dialogue takes place with Candy in 1972 so Mike/Tony was technically correct: the American Psychiatric Association removed homosexuality from the DSM in 1973.

The freedom to express one's true self is an overarching theme that weaves the fragile (and sometimes frayed) tapestry of Abatemarco's *ACTION ITEMS* and, as delivered in *Beautified*, it is heartbreaking. While we know that the playwright's father said "I still love you" when told of his son's love of a man (at the end of *Four Fathers*) and we know that he danced with that adorably awkward boy to the beat of Stonewall (at the end *Cologne*), we learn that brother Mike was handed an entirely different script.

Guided by "well-intentioned but uneducated parents," Mike's mother took her boy by bus from Brooklyn to mid-town Manhattan where he religiously received electro-shock treatments—three times a week for a year—designed to rid him of the gay. The unvarnished portrait that Abatemarco paints is void of touch-ups; the murkier, darker hues expose the undeserving cruelties his big brother withstood, like a trouper. The playwright doesn't psychoanalyze; he empathizes. Empathy: the hallmark of a good playwright.

I may have forgotten to say that Abatemarco is a funny man. Are you laughing yet? He writes zingers and punchlines, applies laugh-out-loud situations and summons characters who exploit their wits to survive. Mike and Candy deliver sophisticated repartee like another unmarried funny couple of yesteryear, Mike and Elaine (Nichols and

May) but their back-and-forth banter is faithfully plot-centric and never constructed in order to achieve X number of guffaws before the first commercial break.

Finally, we meet a couple in *Forever House,* a play that may be less autobiographical but nonetheless captures the zeitgeist of American politics that Abatemarco could not have seen coming unless you believe (as I do) that artists have a subconscious prescient sense of the future.

In the several hundred pages that precede *Forever House*, one sees Abatemarco's herculean struggle to embrace himself, determined to live at peace in his body from this day forward. Wisely, the playwright "pulls his camera back" to provide us with a wider lens that peers into the shifting hot topic of gay marriage. We can surmise, even though this fourth entry in the collection is distanced from real life, Abatemarco is married and has chosen to live in a house, forever, "in sickness and in health, to love and to cherish…"

Jack (just may be a stand-in for Abatemarco) and Ben (could be, just might be, a stand-in for the renowned visual artist Dan McCleary) are discovered in their forever house as the curtain rises, but since there are rarely curtains *per se* in the modern theater where a performance of *Forever House* will likely be performed, you employ your suspension of disbelief and hear the majestic (but often dusty) burgundy fabric rustling as the lights dim.

Forever House is a rambunctious roller coaster ride—double the testosterone, if you dare—transpiring in the 'burbs outside of Los Angeles, where the couple has "assimilated." Ben says, "We're respected now. Free to marry in fifty states." Yet complications arise on nearly every page, beginning with the mysterious apparition of a boy that Jack sees but Ben doesn't, followed by an uninvited appearance of a real estate huckster (a gay drunk whose lines read as if Paul Lynde is delivering them), the arrival of Jack's fabulously prototypical Jewish mama in anticipation of the adoption; the abrupt cancellation of the adoption; an earthquake; a visitation from the Evangelical neighbors next door (the wife, a former Vegas showgirl drug addict); and more madcap antics that sometime overshadow the play's thickening plot.

But Abatemarco's choices are not random; he takes us on a dizzying ride that extends beyond the walls of the house, forever or not, to places that demand that we empathize, not sympathize, with the interior lives of his increasingly lovable, if not always immediately likable, characters.

The play's epiphanous showstopper, "Gayland", delivered by Jack in the final moments of the play, is reminiscent of the feral battlecry of Sondheim's "Rose's Turn" from *Gypsy* in which the character performs a personal inventory in the form of a self- exorcism. Ben has given his partner clear instructions: "Confront your fucking demons."

Just because Abatemarco and his partner had been ensconced in a relationship for thirty-six years at the time of the writing doesn't mean that the demons had lost their power to influence this critical work. How privileged we are that Abatemarco is willing to document the collective sorrow that has continued to affect him while defining the community at large.

Acting the words of Abatemarco, Jack/Tony can't let go of the bashing we first learned about in *Cologne* written in the third person (in all caps): "OR MAYBE IT'S BECAUSE, WHEN HE WAS FOURTEEN, HE WAS JUMPED BY A GANG ON THE PLAYGROUND: 'What are you looking at, faggot?'"

These are the experiences, in real time or metaphorical, that marked thousands upon thousands of us, including Abatemarco's brother Mike. Our playwright has moved from the chart of autobiography to a wider world map that extends beyond the locations traveled in this book to include all communities in peril. On July 7, 2018, the *New*

York Times reported, "Long after Mr. Trump is nothing but a toxic memory, the federal judiciary — from the Supreme Court on down — will bear the smear of his fingerprints."

The only thing to counteract Trump's toxicity is art. Abatemarco's words will thrive, along with the federal judiciary, on the pages of *ACTION ITEMS, Volume I of the Collected Plays of Tony Abatemarco.*

From the moment Abatemarco began his journey as a playwright—when his father died, remember?—until now, has been how many years? And it's not only the number of years, it's how he has packed them—with lessons, revelations, kisses, admissions, confrontations, laughs, confessions—that blossomed into scene after scene that he is willing to share with such utter abandon and remarkable skill. Circling back, we see that death—his father's and his brother's—elicited, if not a rebirth, a reawakening.

We didn't need to experience the pang of losing Justice Kennedy from the Supreme Court to know that the emotional issues Abatemarco dissects with the exactitude of a surgeon have become (and will likely remain for some time) fodder for progressives in L.A. and homophobes in D.C.: abortion, gay marriage, adoption. And we didn't need the magical amalgamation that cements the bond that ties the heartstrings of Jack and Ben—oh, and not to mention Tony and Dan—to each other's unseen souls to know that gay marriage is pure no matter how it is perceived by the court.

Put *ACTION ITEMS* on your must-read list—a book more urgently needed than ever, not only for theater folk, but for anyone who believes that the soaring spirituality of art deserves more votes than the deflating negativity of politics.

Ultimately, Abatemarco was able to defy the "sick" label and any of the other destructive taunts that lingered; instead, he chose to confront his fucking demons. Lucky for us.

Author's Note

Herein lie my first four produced plays.

I chose to call this collection of plays *ACTION ITEMS* because that phrase, so au courant in business circles today, reverberates for me not only as an artistic imperative but as the motivating principle for writing each piece. In that respect, I began each of these plays with a strong impulse to *take action*; through metaphor, through language that investigates and nudges character and circumstance forward, and by extension, to take you on a journey.

In my first two plays, both autobiographical monologues, I was motivated on one hand to memorialize (my dad) and on the other, to exonerate (myself). Strong actions, but neither remain completed in me. Though I've often thought of myself as a eulogist, and sometimes as an apologist, I've learned these efforts at writing my experiences down never fully finalize the processes they initially explored. So be it.

And so, by way of introducing each play's action and as something of a compass to the destination toward which they're headed, I've given each an enumerated signpost. As you read these plays, and how grateful I am you will, a Roman numeral and title will indicate the thematic terrain I set out to explore.

I hope you'll appreciate this authorial device and find pleasure in tracing my impulse to elucidate each theme.

-Tony Abatemarco

I. THE FUTILITY OF HUMAN DEVOTION

FOUR FATHERS
(An Elegy)

Characters:
A single Narrator, male, in a white shirt, black tie and dress slacks.

Setting*:
A bare stage with a large rock, perhaps 60 pounds, which can be
rolled as well as stood on, and a vintage black suit circa '60s style on
a wooden hanger.

*The original Tiffany Theater premiere in Los Angeles in 1993 was
produced by Suzi Dietz & Lenny Beer, directed by Don Amendolia,
stage managed by Sindy Slater, with music by Nathan Birnbaum and
a set by John Nava containing four original oil paintings of mythic
figures and a large fragment of the exterior wall of a single-family
house, including rock and suit, rendered by the artist.*

Production History:
FOUR FATHERS was first presented in a memorial reading by Tony
Abatemarco at Stages Theatre Center in Hollywood in 1992, one year
after the author's father died. A full production was then produced at
The Tiffany Theater, Los Angeles, California for an extended run in
'93, followed by a presentation at Santa Fe Stages, Santa Fe, New
Mexico, both starring the author. It won the '93 DramaLogue Awards
for Best Solo Writing and Performance.

FOUR FATHERS
Tony Abatemarco
(NARRATOR),
Tiffany Theatre
PHOTOS: SINDY SLATER

4

NARRATOR'S PREAMBLE

(Lights up on a bare stage. On stage left sits a single wooden chair. Upstage right sits a large rock the size of a footstool. A vintage black suit hangs upstage center. Enter a NARRATOR in a white shirt and black tie, pants, and shoes.)

I have always pretended my Father was something he was not. As a small child, I thought my Father was a giant. I grew up to be 5'7", looming over his 5'4" frame. Later, I thought he was generous to a fault, until the night we visited the Feast of San Gennaro in New York's Little Italy and I saw him callously brush away the homeless man who begged him for a quarter. Much later still, when I was thirty and living in Los Angeles, he defied my expectations of him again by slipping a ten-dollar bill under the arm of a sleeping drunk. I thought my Father was a lover and defender of equal rights for all until, as a college hippie, I heard him rail against the Black and Puerto Rican takeover of Brooklyn. Yet Black and Puerto Rican men worked for him, some for twenty to thirty years, and were always treated with generosity, thoughtfulness, and respect. I saw them cry at his funeral. I thought he had James Cagney's chutzpah and Clark Gable's brawn and Gene Kelly's graceful charm…until he turned his disapproval on me. Then he was Lon Chaney's *Phantom of the Opera* unmasked: terrifying, vindictive, full of ridicule.

It is one thing to live in opposition to our Fathers: to rebel against everything they are and stand for. To portray them as purveyors of outmoded traditions. To position ourselves *for* what they're positioned *against*. But what happens when time reveals them to be complex men of contradictions, as virtuous or hypocritical as we know ourselves to be? What separates the generations then? And who shall lead and who shall follow? And why are we compelled to still pretend?

In an article from *The New Yorker* by Adam Gopnick, I read this sentence: "We expect our Fathers to take as long a time dying as we took growing up."

FOUR FATHERS was begun immediately after I returned from my Dad's funeral. Born out of a need to keep his history alive. And mine. I had no idea where I was going with it, nor what form it would take. Just as I had no idea how to go on without him. I simply proceeded, week by week, adding memories as they came, building insights into the stony blocks of facts and dates, chiseling through each mask I had concocted for him. It wasn't until the eighth month of mourning that I began to see a metaphorical resonance in this personal tale. And to arrange the data, both factual and emotional, into its present form. It's proved to be an effective way of subverting my fear of the future. I'm prone to that. To looking ahead with too much concern for what's gone. This tale recounts what used to be: My silenced Father, his presence. By speaking I feel his hand extend beyond me, and move on.

> *(Lute music comes up. The Narrator moves to the rock stage right, and with great effort, rolls the rock downstage a few feet. Once in place, he sits upon it.)*

To the ancient Greeks the name "Sisyphus" meant "very wise": a Sun God whose sacred animal was a bull. Sisyphus lived by cunning, and with the way things were back then on Olympus, he went far. He was a God. He was a Dad. He was a sacred King who refused to abdicate at the end of his reign. For this, the Judges of the Dead said, "NO MORE!". They ordered him to roll a huge stone up the face of a hill and topple it down the opposite slope. He has never yet succeeded in doing so. For the hill up which he rolls it is the vault of heaven. As soon as he almost reaches the summit, he is pushed back by the weight of his shameless stone, and must begin again. And so,

Part One:

THE FUTILITY OF HUMAN DEVOTION

SISYPHUS

A few weeks before my Father left this world, he had a mission. His youngest child, a daughter still living at home, was about to be married. For about two years this date had been set, with ample and baroque arrangements put in motion from its very first mention. In the truly ornate manner of Brooklyn-Italian tradition, yards of expensive fabric were ordered and cut, the finest bakeries allocated, a fleet of white stretch limousines with chrome accoutrements was contracted, and the church, City Hall, and a palatial catering fortress were reserved with fat donations slightly padded to ensure a job exceptionally well-done. This was to be, as so many before it have been and so many yet to come will aspire to be, as lavish and ostentatious a function as one man's pride could render. That one man, my Father, hitherto known as *Sisyphus*, could not be underestimated in the pride he held for his daughter, but more importantly, in the pride he held for his lifetime of achievements. Born on Sackett Street, the last of thirteen children to a family of newly-arrived Neopolitan immigrants, whose father was a junk man and enough of an amateur philanderer at some point in his youth to have passed a strain of syphilis down to a few of his children, *Sisyphus* being the last, worst case. So, *Sisyphus*, the sickly child, was given mercury treatments and prescribed a weekly quota of outdoor recreations. By the time he was twelve years old, his athletic prowess and stamina won him a much-competed-for job: Every night he lit the gas lamps of a square mile of South Brooklyn, running all the way.

Each summer was spent at the beach for sun and salt water, when sun and salt water still could heal you. Coney Island. Out of this baroque milieu, with its questionable benefits of amusement and health, a powerfully-muscled dynamo with federalistic proclivities was evolving into the patriarch, Dad.

For his sixty-fifth birthday, Dad put friends and family, some doddering, some diapered, on the Coney Island Carousel—"Just us. No Strangers."—and paid the man for an extended ride. Standing off. "What's he doing?" "Watching us spin." That was his retirement party. He went back to work the next day. Does every life have a place that resounds with as much significance as Coney Island did for my Dad? Coney Island, where every July and August, our scantily-clad progenitors exposed their lust-crazed limbs to the indiscriminate sun and the prurient appraisal of prospective companions. I rode the 2 train there last summer and saw an American ruin as vivid as any Parthenon or Coliseum. Does anyone remember, care, pay homage to their Coney Island, Sackett Street, Prospect Park, Brooklyn? The spawning ground of our country, where until recently, one out of every four Americans was born. My Father, *Sisyphus*, never did not recognize his antiquated borough as a power-piston generator to our workforce grit.

    (*A phone rings and he answers as his Father.*)
"Hello, A&A Brake Service."

"Hi Dad. What are you doing?"

"Working. What are you doing, picking oranges off the trees? When are you gonna give up that rat race and come home to me and reality?"

As luck would have it, his youngest daughter had optioned to get married to a boy whose family had remained intact in the Fatherland, Oh, Bountiful shores, Oh, Brooklyn! The big day approached and RSVPs came pouring in. "Yes," they said mostly, while the few who declined sent money. Dad kept ledgers of who came to what weddings and what they gave dating back to 1944, so you can bet that people were attentive to the summons of old *Sisyphus*, whose last daughter would be witnessed, worthy, in her white lace wedding gown, to walk fidelity's plank to the alter. I too made my libations, sacrificed a calf, had my suit dry cleaned, and booked my flight from Los Angeles with the courage and conviction of no possible rain checks, two months in advance.

(*Sound of thunder.*)

It is now mid-spring, temperamentally November though my watch says April 5th. An idea condensing in the brain of an old man has biblical proportions, like a mountain. Like the sky getting ready for a cumulonimbus when the weather was serene just an inning or two before.

We pause now to genuflect in homage to the last of several projects to engulf my Father's mind.

(*He mimes turning TV channels by remote control.*)

With the Angel/Maiden/Girl upstairs he turns the channel… vacantly, the remote limp in his hand. A thorn of a thought is lodged in his mind, and he's focusing intently on that dot. The Angel/Maiden/Girl is busy with details of her wedding in the apartment he built for her upstairs. An apartment that has grown from two tiny attic rooms to a full floor of spacious living quarters with a deck of poured concrete, mounted high above his porch, trellised with a pattern of white iron leaves, and crenulated Old New Orleans style. Nothing is too good for that Angel/Maiden/ Girl; that proud, determined honor roll inductee. Schooled in Boston. National Oratory Prize recipient. No act is too flashy for her passage up the aisle to where each Sunday she reads sermon. And the choirs of his feeling sing:

(*He sings.*)

ANGEL/MAIDEN/GIRL

WHAT CARPET CAN I ROLL BENEATH YOUR FEET?

MY PRIDE SUFFERS TO RELEASE YOU

WHAT BLOOD FACT CAN I LAY OUTSIDE THE THRESHOLD

OF THE STRONG KNOT PACT THAT WILL BIND YOU TO A

LOVER

FOR A WOMAN/MOTHER/WIFE LIFE TOGETHER?

And the dot takes shape, and the idea fills the sky of his cranium. It's going to pour. *Sisyphus* has climbed abundant hills with his tough rocks; he knows how it's accomplished. Take action. With a heave and a ho, he resolves to tar the driveway by his own strength: a prodigious assignment for a man of twenty-one. But nothing is too good for his Angel/Maiden/Girl, and one Saturday, the Hardware is approacheth.

    (*In his Father's voice.*)

"I'm looking for tar. Thirty gallons. Six large cans. Can you help me, Miss?"

Graciously, tar is ordered. For that is how old *Sisyphus* accomplished all he did. Civility disarmed and apprehended. What was never clarified, I daresay never spoken, was the *type* of tar required for a driveway. Chalk it up to certainty, to age, to other matters, the fact is that *roofing tar* arrived with some dispatch, and an old man worked steadfastly applying it. To have witnessed the diligent techniques of this work wizard in all his other ventures was to appreciate meticulousness in action. So brilliantly accomplished was his surety of hand that his home was a veritable Epcot habitat. Circuits reinvented. Gardening tools refined. Watering systems time-released and measured. A toilet tank system with adjustable flush, which employs "a lighter setting for eliminating urine." To the challenges of civic engineering he contributed a more efficient bus door. A paraplegic's auto controls; hand-operated brake and gas, adaptable to any chassis. These were just a few of the countless "works improvements" he realized in his passion for precision. Why, even the air brakes on the Rockaway roller coaster were installed by this old man. Much younger. In spare time. In time made spare by efficiency. We, his meeker progeny, have other coarse ambitions: wordsmithing, hairdressing, head-shrinking, registering Democrat. Nay, not *Sisyphus*. Not granite-molded *Sisyphus*. A Thomas Hart Benton mural of a man. This twentieth-century turbo-powered epoch gave reign to his brawn par excellence.

(*Thunder again. A tremendous downpour.*)

And the rains came. And the tar never dried. Nay, it moveth as the ancient river Jordan. Unto sidewalks, unto streets, where the passing traffic tracked it like a squid-stained blemish pointing that way, back to *his* house. The house of *Sisyphus*. There he is! He's the one! Blame him! *Sisyphus* in horror, *Sisyphus* contrite, at the living room window watching God take over. Trading a deluge for my Father's hard work gift. Mocking him. Throwing him a bone.

(*The voice of God.*)

"Fetch it. Stay. Sit. Nice man. Roll over. Roll that stone. Heavier. Unbearable."

An idea is a black dog is a last shot at grace, Thou shalt not save face, Thou shalt fall apart, with a blood clot, with a blood clot, with a blood clot in the heart. This fist is a last sign of a son's defiance, thrown like a stone, at your steeple, God. Not a gift, God. A fist, God. My stone. Defiance. I shalt not forget thy cruelty! Remember *Sisyphus*! My Dad.

Did my Father's fixation with godliness kill him? Just two weeks later he was hooked up to life support. Maybe not. The tar incident was just another bead on his long rosary of contritions. This is the other way many men pray. The cathartic benediction of hard labor. But the monumental suffering to surpass himself, and by his progress, glorifying God…does it end with him? Am I dying to honor my Father, or am I living to better him? Are you out there in the dark with a stone in your heart, pushing uphill, competing? Did you lose a Dad, too, or never knew you had one? Doesn't it seem like everyone is Fatherless these days? Is there a dialogue in the house? Or is this just one more *one-man show*? No!

> (*Raucous music up. He dances wildly, finally coming to a stop. He sits.*)

There are so many stories of King Zeus, the Father of Heaven, and so many aspects of this thunderbolt-wielding gigolo that I am hard-pressed to single out one. But his relationship to one of his first sons, Hermes, is what now comes to mind. We know Hermes as Mercury. I knew him as a chrome plaque on the side of our car. A disembodied head with wings on his helmet: Lincoln-Mercury. I'll come to that.

Art was among the provinces of Hermes' special skills. He made beautiful, spectral music as an infant. From a tortoise shell. He was also quite a trickster, which did his Father proud, and nearly did him in on one occasion. When Zeus murdered a mortal woman in her sixth month of pregnancy for carrying his illegitimate child, it was Hermes who saved the fetus by implanting it in Zeus's thigh, bringing the baby to term three months later. Childlike himself, Hermes guaranteed safe passage, and as herald of Hell, gently hailed the dying: I've always identified with Hermes, with Mercury. Mercurial. I love change. I love playing midwife to special projects. I love to drive, and sometimes, to be driven.

Part Two:
THE BIRTH OF THE MESSENGER
HERMES, THE SON OF ZEUS

(*The Narrator moves the chair to stage center and sits.*)
For a full year after my Mother died, I spent many hours in the car with my Dad. In other locations as well, which we got to in our Lincoln Continental. One of our more frequent destinations was St. Charles Cemetery in Farmingdale, Long Island. It was fairly new then, in 1964, set on a vast tract of well-landscaped terrain. Peaceful, as a cemetery should be. My Mother's grave was in Section 13, a quiet, moderately-populated corner. Her stone was pink, her favorite

color, carved with roses, a cross, and a scroll. SAY ONE HAIL MARY was inscribed along the bottom, with her name, ROSE, and life dates beneath that. 1912-1963. Dad was a Sunday-service man. Very devoted. When he was twenty or twenty-one, and keeping company with the girl he loved, my Mother, he cut himself moving a large rusty chain at work. They told him that he'd have to have his left pointer finger removed due to a gangrenous infection that was developing and he promised God that if my Mother still loved him he would put two dollars away a week for the church. And she did. And he did. All his life. His name's on a plaque at St. Bernard's in Brooklyn. "Benefactor." Mom, on the other hand, only went to Mass on Easter Sunday, and then, primarily to show off her latest spring hat. Nevertheless, I'm sure he would have had no qualms about the religious motif Dad chose for her resting place. His resting place, too. Twenty-eight years later. And Grandma's resting place. And who knows who's to come? There are nine more spaces in it, though none of us are inclined to lay down beside our parents under roses, a cross, and a scroll. I did lay down beside my Dad one time. For the week after Mom died, Dad had me sleep beside him in their bed, underneath their wedding cross. A large wooden replica of the crucified Christ with a copper Jesus tearfully suspended. Like the two of us, also tearfully suspended on the meeting point of our criss-crossed grief. It was a grief built solidly on the ruins of an existence that, even to this day, appears golden. The High Renaissance of our family. The years, 1956-1963: I'm not equipped to talk about the quality of life for the middle-class American back then. I was a child. Despite precociousness, I saw life through the filter of familial protection and a color TV—first one on the block! But in memory, the palace of minutiae was embossed with a sparkling veneer of favorite pastimes. Dad collected records; diamond needles, golden throats: "Ella in Berlin," Brubeck's "Time Out," "Lambert, Hendricks and Ross," "The Hi-Lo's." Mom washed, waxed, basted, broiled, bounteously. My brother and my sister were comparing gems, engaged, and adjusting hems and gestures for their trousseaus. I slept with Grandma, who lived with us since when? The Depression? Her blind husband died? Forever. In her satin nightgowns and clouds of lilac powder, she'd envelop me with ample pats and kisses. Sunday was a feast day we'd celebrate together, from waking up with the smell of meatballs frying for the sauce to the order of TV shows watched religiously at night: "Lassie," by myself; Disney's "Wonderful World of Color," with Grandma; "Bonanza," Dad and Mom joined in; and finally, "Candid Camera," with the whole clan rounding off the day. And the trips in the car, those local excursions to see relatives and friends, were transcendental.

(*He chants, rhythmically.*)

THAT SATURDAY NIGHT IN THE LINCOLN
TOWN CAR, BEAUTIFUL PERFECT MACHINE
MOM, DAD, MIKE AND LANA AND

17

GRANDMA, AND OF COURSE, ME.
EVERYONE BRUSHED AND TALCED AND SCENTED
EVERYONE FACING FRONT EXPECTANT
I AM THE MOST ALERT I HAVE BEEN,
A CHILD ON A PAR WITH ADULTS.
IN THE BACK RIGHT SEAT MY FEET
DON'T TOUCH THE FLOOR OF THE CAR.
I DON'T CARE MUCH. THE QUALITY
OF MY ADULT CONVERSION IS STRICTLY,
IN MY VIEW, SUCCEEDING.
ADEPT-ADULT. ADEPT-ADULT. THE CAR,
DAD'S DRIVING. OUR CLOSENESS.
THAT UNIFIED MOMENT IN SOME CHILDREN'S LIVES
WHEN EVERY PERCEPTION SIZZLES.
SATURDAY NIGHT. SILVERY LIGHT.
"DON'T HUG ME, GRANDMA. HERE DAD,
TURN RIGHT." WE ARE A MOTHER SHIP–
HERMETICALLY TIGHT—FLYING OUR FLAG
ON STRANGE WATERS. THE CURRENT
OF TRAFFIC HAS SHIFTED AGAINST US.
"WITH TRAFFIC THIS BAD, THERE MUST
BE AN ACCIDENT," OUR CAPTAIN, MY FATHER,
INFORMS US. "I KNOW THAT, DAD,"
I SAY TO MYSELF. I CAN'T WAIT 'TIL I

GET MY LICENSE. AT EIGHT, OR NINE, OR
TEN–WAS I TEN?–THAT INFINITE INTERVAL
GALLED ME. I'M BUSY INVENTING A JET-
PROPELLED CAR WITH VERTICAL TAKE-OFF
OPTIONS, WHEN WE MOVE ADJACENT
TO DAD'S PRESCIENT GUESS. THERE,
JUST OFF MY SIDE, THE PILE-UP:
(*The speed of his chanting increases.*)
AMBULANCE, COP CAR, PERPETRATOR,
VICTIMS. EVERYBODY BUSY
ASSISTING, WHEN SUDDENLY "LADY"
IN PASSENGER'S SEAT SLIDES LEFT
TOWARDS DRIVER'S DOOR, HOPING
TO EXIT THE WRECK WITHOUT BRUISES
OR MAYBE JUST ONE FOR THE LAWYERS.
MISPLACING HER FOOT ON THE BROKEN CAR'S
GAS, SHE CATAPULTS IT INTO TRAFFIC.
I'M STANDING AND WATCHING, REAR
WINDOW, RIGHT SIDE. THE BROKEN IMPALA
PROJECTILE IS SUDDENLY SMILING ITS GRILLWORK
OF TEETH AT MY THROAT, AND
LEAPING LIKE TROUT AT THE BUTTERFLY LURE
OF MY QUIZZICAL FACE, ITS TARGET.
BAM! INTO LINCOLN AND SHUDDER AND

19

STOP! WHILE I'M IN SLOW-MOTION WHIRLPOOL.

SOMERSAULT. SOMERSAULT. SOMERSAULT

DOWN. NOT EVEN INJURED. RELEASED.

(*He resumes at a slower pace.*)

SOME ASSAULTS ARE BETTER THAN CANDY

WHEN YOU'RE IN THE FAMILY FOLD.

THE CAR WAS STILL DRIVABLE.

DAD DID THE PAPERWORK. GRANDMA

KEPT HUGGING ME. "THANK YOU." AND OFF

INTO SATURDAY SAILED OUR BATTALION,

ADEPT ADULTS. ONE CHILD

FOR ONCE I APPRECIATE MY STATUS: "BABY."

FLEXIBLE BONES. BIG HUGS.

(*He rises, crosses upstage to where the black suit hangs.*)

That was the coddling crib I grew up in. Bundled in love. No brag.

Dad loved Mom and Mom loved back. Palpably so. I witnessed.

(*Putting on the jacket.*) Mom gave Dad this suit for their anniversary.

1960. And now, my prayer for the lost love shared by my parents:

(*Chanting—Gregorian style.*)

IN EARLY 1930s HE FOLLOWS HER HOME

WALKING WITH HER SISTER

WON'T GO AWAY

IN 1934 HE MARRIES HER

HIS MOTHER AND HIS BROTHER CHECK THE SHEETS THE
NEXT DAY
"SHE'S A VIRGIN?" "YES." THEY LEAVE CONTENT
IN TWENTY-NINE YEARS, BAD AND GOOD, THREE KIDS
BORN
NO ONE DIES
MOVED FROM CITY HOUSE, BRICKS AND BROWN
OUT TO THE SUBURB HOUSE, PINK AND GRAY
GOLDEN AGE OF THEIR FAMILY NOW
HEALTH, PROSPERITY, TWO KIDS WED
JAZZ ON THE STEREO
BEAUTIFUL MEALS
STYLE AND CONTENT
HOLIDAYS GRAND
TRIP TO FLORIDA LAST GREAT FLING
HER OPERATION, EARLY SPRING
HOPEFUL RECOVERY, FAST DETERIORATION
AUGUST 27th, 1963
SHE DIES AT HOME WITH HER FAMILY CLOSE
MOANING
"MOMMY"
HE BECOMES RECLUSIVE, RESPONSIBLE, REMOTE
WALKS IN LATE, PAYS BILLS, EATS OUT
SELLS OFF PROPERTY

TIGHTENS HIS BELT

CARRIES HER BODY IN HIS BROKEN HEART

WON'T FORGET HER

RARELY TALKS

LONGINGLY

CAN'T FORGIVE ANYTHING

Anyway, lots of time was spent traveling around that year. Side by side. Me and Dad. My Captain. Not too much was said, but in that "not too much," everything was said. Once or twice, "big themes" got discussed; the "Facts of Life" discussion was the weirdest: "Remember when your sister used to live at home, and sometimes she'd get so crabby she'd stay in her pajamas all day long, and do that 'rocking' motion at the table? Well…" This was not the Never Never Land of Sex I'd always dreamed of. We were, however, Lost Boys; Mom was dead of…"causes". "Don't fall asleep, Dad. Steer me." Dad prayed in the car. On his way to work, every morning, he would dip his head each time he mouthed a silent "Jesus," cross himself each time we passed a church. This left me time to think about the devil: Marilyn Monroe in *Some Like It Hot*, Burt Lancaster in *From Here to Eternity*. The Beatles. The night the Beatles were on Ed Sullivan, Dad made a confession. It was a few months since Mom died. We were at her sister's new house. Me, my cousin, and my mother's two sisters went for a ride in the Lincoln. Dad drove. Drinks were drunk and tongues were loose and Dad confessed infidelities to the two surviving sisters of his recently buried wife. Tears were shed and kindnesses offered in condolence. But I…I sat, remote, in the back right seat, my chest contracting: "Adept adult. Adept adult. Adept adult…adulterer."

(Sings "All My Loving" by The Beatles.)

The Bowling Club Weekend! An annual event. Dad had been President for years, and each summer a large group of his Bowling Club friends would head out to some northeast resort for three days of fun and games, with their families, in some cases. More often, just husband and wife. In this case, this year, Dad and me. A widowed man with a twelve-year-old son gets a lot of attention from his friends, and *Zeus* was no exception. Yes, *Zeus* is whom I am talking about now. Finally. The god who consorted with mortals to his nearest of kins' chagrin. *Zeus* stands alone in the mud by the pond, watching kids slay frogs with a bow and arrow. Is his mind wandering to that young swan in the meadow? Will he take her as his wife and retain his manly form, or become the dragon-snake of my kindergarten nightmare? I watch him watch her and my mind is splitting sideways. It has been a year of watching shifting clouds for signs of Mom, and fathers cast long shadows when they mourn too near their sons. There he is! That's my Dad. No, wait, this is a changing, alien god mutating before my eyes. "No, Dad, don't be gruff. I'm not adult. Don't take the coo out of your 'How's my boy?'." I'm confused. Just yesterday he woke me from a nap in our

23

motel room with: "See this bed you're sleeping in? That's where you were conceived." How can I put these primal facts together? I'm not ready. I'm too green. I take a walk. I leave the grounds. I'M BAD. I am now hidden in the low brush, hot. I crawl to sand pits, burning. I'M TWELVE. My body is going mad. My mother and father, in love forever, are coiling round my legs. Their love is squeezing all of my blood into my swollen tongue. Warm sun bleaching iris open. Infant flesh discarded. Baby-faced and serpent-tailed, I chew roots and chant: Puberty, Puberty, Puberty, Puberty, Savage me, Rescue me, Take me! I will make monuments of my mouth mirth.

    (*He crosses the stage, reptile-like.*)

"Waaa! Waaa! Ha-Ha-Ha! Cocksucker / Motherfucker, KILL!" Slowly. Rising. Out of the dust of a dry terrain, I spot one box turtle. I had a series of turtles once. A repetition of reptiles. A repetition of little lives gone out with short, sharp pangs. I am a soldier that vindicates all the infractions I'm feeling. Slowly. Rising. Towering. Deft. I am a soldier that mutilates helpless unarmed wild things. Diving. Strafing. Bellicose. Blind. I will not let another thing I care for die from "causes".

    (*With violent, chopping strokes.*)

I AM THE CAUSE! I AM THE CAUSE! I AM THE CAUSE! Amen.

That night I swallow a fifth of rye and vomit for twenty-two hours.
The catharsis is complete. Manhood is conceived. Now I wear a
hollow mask with whiskers and black tongue. *Zeus*? He doesn't
recognize the change in me. He's driving. His mask says:

> (*Holding one arm up.*)

"I lost my wife." Mine says:

> (*Holding the other arm up.*)

"I spilled blood." We keep our secrets to ourselves, there is no
forgiveness. Slowly. Rising. Totem. Tribe.

> (*The Troggs' "Wild Thing," the original version, comes up.*
> *With arms lifted, the Narrator sways in time to the music as*
> *lights fade nearly to black, then abruptly brighten. He drops*
> *the incantational gesture, crosses down to the audience.*)

Here's a radical idea. Your parents die and it has nothing to do with
you. Your Mom's breast cancer is not a result of your continued need
to suck on that tit well into your thirties and forties. Her malignant
tumors are not a metaphor for the children like you, or better, her
body can no longer bear.

Your Dad's heart attacks or his emphysema are not the culmination of
his infinite disappointment in your inability to respect his opinion.
His stroke didn't come because you're out of work, you didn't
become a dentist, you're a deadbeat Dad yourself, or divorced, in

debt, a homo. Their lives are simply over. No metaphor. They're through.

I guess if you really hate your parents, or never really knew them, this way of thinking may not be alien to you.

"Eww, what? Those two jerks? They smoked and drank themselves to death. Their idea of good parenting was 'children should be seen, not heard.'" Generally Italians don't fall under this category. Anyway, I don't. Which brings us to THE PEOPLE WHO HAGGLE WITH THEIR PARENT'S DEATH—a subdivision of the Death-Obsessed—among whom I am.

A great industry has sprung up catering to the needs of people like me, with living trusts, estate planning, inheritance taxes, etc. Certainly, those most active in grappling with Mr. Grim Reaper, second only to those about to die, are we, the Bereaved.

For example, take this watch. (*He holds it up.*) An ordinary instrument. Quartz. Seiko. The Estate watch. Part of my Father's personal effects that I, youngest son, had access to when, you know, he… Nothing unique except that I talk to my watch. You may think that odd, the talking-to. Time is the only answer that comes back, after all. But, it is a continuum I'm the most concerned with when addressing my watch. It only verifies that Time and Dad are synonymously linked, contained, remembered. Every day now my pulse has regulations to adhere to, strict shackles to the pound of what previously amounted to an infinite number of heartbeats. They'll stop one day. I know that now. My watch says:

(*He holds the watch up to his ear and intones.*)

Tick – Tick – Tick – Tick – THINK – THIS – THROUGH –
'TIL – TRUTH – COMES – TRUE – Tick – YOU – ARE – NOT
WHAT – KILLED – ME.

(*To watch.*)

Who? – Dad – Who – Then?

Tick – Tick – Tick – Tick –

(*From watch.*)

I – DID. – I – DIED. – Tick – Tick – Tick – Tick – Tick –
RE – MEM – BER ME!

Part Three:

COVERT ALLEGIANCES

HAMLET AND THE KING, HIS GHOSTLY FATHER

We lived on Covert Avenue. Really. A picturesque corner lot with a landscaped and manicured lawn. Our moat. We remained in that house for nearly two years after Mom's death. Then it was sold and our nuclear family began its endless splitting. A wildness had set in, upsetting the order of my regulated life and to match it, I randomly selected different ties. (*He undoes his tie, sits on the floor.*) Summer nights were suddenly marauded by stampedes of teenage girls galloping through the neighborhood. We boys would lay out eerily past nine or ten o'clock on damp lawns, waiting. Whispering: "I wish…I want…I wonder…" When underneath the streetlights a hint of sneakered feet came rumbling across the night, and perfume…we barely kept our writhing in check as they approached, their strangely tinted manes swished with silver. It wasn't long before we rose and followed them to homes with dark dens, and absentee fathers. Donna Baciamento, whose father was in jail, had a mother who enjoyed teasing hair. Her house became the clubhouse, all hours, every day. A sort of Motown make-out pad of hormonal groping. A seething competition of obsession and rejection and release and resist and "How far did you go?" kept unfolding, and I found myself unworthy, all too unworthy for the first time in my life, with unwieldy propositions far beyond me. So I ripped myself free of those people who had loved me. I went to military school and earned "Salutatorian—7th Grade." By now, Dad remarried. All was changed. He didn't come to pick me up that graduation day. Too busy. My two bright gold medals dangled, worthless. So I set out to conquer the world that he'd ignored. A world of letters. Speeches. Academia. I pinned things to my shirtfront that he could never own. Eloquence. Psychology. Man-love. And I went as public as a lettered man could go with a virulent belief in independence. Half of my life's hemisphere is armored with awards. (*He puts one hand on a hip.*) This other half still reaches. (*He does.*) Recognition. For twenty-seven years I didn't give up hope that there might be some medallion that he prized. Familiar? "You'll never fill your Father's shoes," my cousin Gerry gloated.

Two years ago I shined the shoes my father bought in Ireland. The beautiful black boots he wore in his coffin. Just three months before, he had worn them to the opening of my directorial debut at The Kennedy Center. That night he sat behind me; ill, gray, old. His doctor had said, "Don't get out of bed." But there he sat, behind me, stifling a cough that was threatening to disrupt our rapt attention. I could hear him wheezing. I could hear the clenching of his lips in strict suppression of each spasm of his strangulated breath. He never let it happen. He honored what I'd done. I hold that golden medal in my heart.

(*He holds the watch up to look at it again.*)

Tick – Tick – Tick – Tick – Dad – Is – Not – Sick

Dad – Is – Too – Quick – To – Be

– TICK!

(*Sounds of an enormous thunder, and lights flashing. He falls to the floor, and speaks in the booming voice of his Father.*)

"HOW DARE YOU THINK YOU CAN SPEAK FOR ME?! YOU VIOLATE MY REST! YOU'RE ALWAYS AT THE CENTER OF ATTENTION! THIS IS NOT ABOUT YOU! I AM NOT YOUR LIFE! 'REMEMBER ME' DOES NOT MEAN 'BECOME ME'! RELEASE ME! I'M WARNING YOU. *I* GOT SICK. I'M FINISHED! MAKE YOUR OWN BED! LIE IN IT!"

(*He rises, shaken, brushes himself off, speaks to the heavens.*) Do I have the strength to "remember," not "become"? Isn't anyone to blame for that poisonous breath of death in your ear that whispered, "Ready or not, here I come"? I'd blame them.

Can I look at how you died and stay separate? Can I stand beside your body, kept alive by those machines, and allow "intensive care" to console you? Can't I just hold on and deliver you to Heaven, spend an afternoon attending to your comfort, so that someone can come back with that most assuring news, "He's alright. His room's nice. There's a window by his bed, beyond which is a carousel…always turning."

(*He moves to another area of the stage.*) Daedalus, the great craftsman, made the heinous mistake of tricking the gods, twice. For his punishment, a mortal king imprisoned him along with his son, Icarus, in a high tower above the sea. Shrewdly, he gathered the quills of pens and fashioned two great sets of wings with the wax of so many candles. Icarus watched his father well.

Listened to his instructions. "Follow my flight, but don't digress. The sun will melt these wings." And so together, late one night, they flew the coop. Free, ascending, ecstatic. But Icarus wanted proof of Heaven. And just then, the Sun...

Part Four:
THE RENDEZVOUS OF SPIRITS
ICARUS AND DAEDALUS

(*He returns to the rock, sits, takes a worn piece of paper out of his pocket, reads.*)

The practical things have lost their model
Now that my Father is gone.
The carved-in-wood things, etched-in-stone things,
Chrome, steel, copper...

The physical world has lost its mentor.
Laces knot irretrievably, towels fray,
And even sheets that once obeyed
The body's contours smoothly
Now nightly tear and wrangle
In ragged accompaniment to dreams.
The useful things have lost their meaning,
A surrogate role replacing each tacit task, design,

And mourning groans its luckless tone

Along surfaces, beneath.

Shoes, even, don't know why

And return listlessly to closets.

The adaptable things have lost their mirth

Just doing what is required. Nothing extra.

No wide margins. Not elastic. Stiff.

The mechanical things have lost momentum

Or regained some autonomy

That predates any association

With Anthony, Daedalus, Dad.

My world whirls, inevitably.

A shocking recognition to have practical things perform

Without model, meaning, mirth.

(*He puts the paper away.*)

I wrote that one month after my father's life became a medical record, its history contained in a file I could lift and thumb through with one hand. Listlessly. There was no other way to turn those pages, where words like PATIENT and CARDIAC and ARREST weighed in with equal gravity. It is here that Coney Island closes its parenthetical frame around that life lived seventy-eight years. Sackett Street is where he was born. Sackett Street is where he grew up. Sackett Street is where he built his shop and worked 'til his last day of consciousness. But Coney Island is the place we return to perform the functions of farewell. Entering into those eight days of extinguishment, exhausting and extenuating, Extreme Unction days, from the first phone call…"He's at Coney Island Hospital, Tony. It's bad." Booking the red-eye out of LAX, and all the way through to the other side, to the yellow-cab ride back out of Brooklyn, with a welcomed, anonymous driver who didn't know my circumstance and couldn't have cared less. He had his hot black coffee, "to go," to balance, and the wheel, and his repertoire of "Give me Brooklyn any day." Why should he care what I'd been through, or whom I prayed for silently?

(*He becomes the cab driver.*)

"Hey, didja hear the one about the guy who moved to L.A. on a bet? He lost! Ha-ha-ha-ha. Ha-ha-ha-ha, ha-ha-ha-ha, sucker!"

(*He taps his chest, mea-culpa style.*)

PATIENT

(*Tap tap.*)

CARDIAC

(*Tap tap.*)

ARREST

(*Tap tap.*)

To experience the glaring fluorescent night of a hospital waiting room…to make what private, transportable serenities you can out of the overcrowded mayhem and overlapping sorrows…to stare into the darkened eyes of an overworked doctor, an overwrought nurse, an over-preening receptionist, hoping to make sense out of the subterfuge, the jargon, the carefully placed phrases that you're meant to comprehend, but they have to be repeated over and over 'cause you never dared to dream you'd have to listen to them said. "And what _are_ you saying, 'brain dead'? Are you saying 'no chance'? Are you Satan?! I'll sue you, you son of a bitch. I'll show you a visitor's pass. I'll shove that fucking clipboard down your…"

(*He calms himself.*)

PATIENT

(*Tap tap.*)

CARDIAC

(*Tap tap.*)

ARREST.

A rest. A private, transportable serenity. And you look at him. It is as if a tall tower has been constructed out of the flesh of your father. He has been stretched to accommodate the circuitry, the dials, the gadget of sustained imprisonment, but he is a man who would leap, if given the chance. If the High Court of Heaven would extend that final wish, he would back up several steps for good leverage, run, and fly! You must have seen that happen. That meteoric leap? Someone you have known ascending. FLASH!!! I want to see him do it. I want these wires twisted into unsalvageable debris. I want a crater left where this hospital bed stands, and plaques with his name decorating Brooklyn. I saw this man run through life. Leaping…Landing…Leaping.

Lana, my sister, nine years old hit by a truck. There's Dad leaping the fence. Like a force of nature with pistons for calves, punching that arrogant driver. That's him leaping into action at work. Showing his workers how. Leaning his back into all kinds of challenges. Leaping with pain and dignity out of the black hole left by Mother's passing. And there, in the ocean, way out past the surf. Leaping. Laughing. Leaping. Waving.

"I want to do that, too. Let my limbs get strong like that! Let me! Look, I'm learning. Lift me, too! Lift me!!"

And I board the plane. The practical thing. The weightless contraption lifts me. Departure. Departing. Departed. Dead. Daedalus, motioning skyward. The prison of grief is shrinking fast. What will I remember?

> (*Suddenly his father is heard singing an old Italian tune. As the song ends.*)

Yes, I remember that, Dad. We were locked in a tower where we were forced to dream. And we dreamed Escape. The attendant kept saying, "Visiting hours are over, Sir. Visiting hours are done." But we had something more to say before they cut you up again. Before they reached inside your chest to install their latest gauge. You, the great Craftsman, who dared too much, and I, your apprentice, who believed you. Yes, I remember how you said, "Let's confess," and I did. I told you about the man I love, and you said, "I still love you." And how you watched me fasten that cherished feather to my arm. And how we turned each other's heartache over in our hands, relieved to know mistakes were made. Relieved to be forgiven. And yes, I saw that single cloud above our house when Mom died…the vertical one where, we all knew, her spirit left its trace. Yes, I want to go there now. I do see how. Just lift them. This way. (*He holds his arms akimbo.*) I won't get lost. I'll follow. (*Nodding his head, repeating a lesson.*) "Too low, we're caught. Too high, they melt." I understand. Let's do it. Ready? On your mark. Get set. Go.

(*The lights and music segue. He speaks as if flying.*)
Dad, I can see the beach from here. The Wonder Wheel. The Cyclone. Dad, don't fall asleep on me. Steer me. Steer me! Here, turn left, turn right. Thanks. Thanks, Dad. Thank you, Dad. Thank you. Look, the sun…the sun is out! Thank you for the sun!

(*Music swells. He smiles. Lights fade to black.*)

END OF PLAY.

II.   THE PERILS OF PASSING

COLOGNE
or, *The Ways Evil Enters The World*

Characters:
A single Narrator, male, age 35 to 50.

Setting:
A simple set comprised of four free-standing, evenly spaced wood paneled flats upstage of a narrow platform that runs left to right, downstage of which lie three bright green AstroTurf carpets, a wicker chair stage right, and a small wooden trunk containing a high school yearbook, the *Beatles '65* album cover, a few yards of brocaded fabric, and a spray bottle of Jade East cologne. The design combines a "Kabuki theater" look with a 1960s den.

Production History:
COLOGNE was first presented in a workshop at Highways Performance Space in Santa Monica under the direction of David Schweizer in 1999. In 2000 it received its world premiere at the Tiffany Theatre in West Hollywood, produced by Paula Holt and Eileen T'Kaye and stage managed by Jeff Cain, with a set by Dan McCleary. After an extended run, it then opened at Theater 150 in Ojai, California in 2001, followed by a run at the Evidence Room in Los Angeles. In 2002, it opened in Santa Fe, New Mexico in a festival of three gay-themed events including David Sedaris and Lea Delaria. In July of that year it transferred to the Rattlestick Theatre Off Broadway, with the same directing and design team, produced by Holt, T'Kaye and Suzi Dietz in association with David Van Asselt and Rattlestick. Future productions were included at the Lavender Footlights Festival in Miami, Florida, and under the author's dirction starring Harry Hart-Browne at the Santa Monica Playhouse and Skylight Theatre in 2010.

Author's Note: Any actor cast as Narrator is encouraged to substitute his own name wherever 'Tony' is mentioned.

COLOGNE
Tony Abatemarco (NARRATOR),
Tiffany Theatre
PHOTOS: MARTIN COHEN

(*Pre-set lights. A simple set: upstage, a wood-paneled wall. On the floor, three bright identical area rugs. One chair, stage right. Down left, a small trunk on the floor. These elements should all suggest furnishings popular in the '60s, with a hint of the Kabuki theatre.*

As lights dim, a man—the NARRATOR—*enters carrying a flashlight. Scanning the space, he illuminates the trunk stage left. Stage lights brighten as he crosses to the trunk, kneels before it and tentatively opens the lid, from which a gust of incense smoke emerges. He explores the contents of the trunk, including a high school yearbook, a vintage Beatles album cover, and finally, a small cologne atomizer of Jade East. He sniffs it, eyes widening, and turns towards the audience.*)

NARRATOR

(*To audience.*)

1965: "BOBBY."

(*A bell chimes.*)

Bobby wasn't pretty, nor was he especially bright. He was older, having just completed his senior year of high school, and there was something proud and feral about him that elevated his status among the younger boys splashing around his pool that day. Especially to Tony. To Tony, Bobby Crane was a man.

(He settles on the rug.)

It had been announced earlier that Bobby might show up. His younger brother, Billy, had intimated to his friends that Bobby might be coming down for a swim.

It was early summer and the pool, twelve feet in diameter, was the largest of its kind in the development. The development itself was a suburban enclave of thirty-two split-level houses built quickly and efficiently along a farm road sixty miles outside of Manhattan. Despite the fact that it lay midway between the glittering towers of the city and the aristocratic porches of the Hamptons, this part of Long Island resembled Iowa.

The town's center lay two miles away, adjacent to a state-run asylum, and it was there that most of its inhabitants found employment. Bobby and Billy's father, Mr. Crane, was an electrician at the "nut house." That's how they liked to put it when out of earshot of their Dad, a dour man with a zest for whipping straps. There were six brothers in their family, and they lived in the filthiest house on the block, in the development, in the town, in Suffolk County, on immaculate Long Island, New York.

Billy Crane was by far the smartest, most talented, and most droll member of his family. He was also a weakling with thick-lensed

42

glasses, but he shared with Tony, his best friend on the block, a serious preoccupation: Beatlemania.

Meet the Beatles! was their hitching post, shared lyric by lyric and lick by lick at the bus stop before school, and with each successive album their friendship deepened. This summer, they rhapsodized over *Beatles '65*. Tony was fourteen, Billy sixteen. Sex was all that mattered to them. Sex and the Beatles.

Ecstasy.

By some happy coincidence, six boys showed up to inaugurate the Cranes' pool that early July afternoon. No girls. The boys ruled.

The pool roiled and foamed with inner-tube attacks fueled by spectacular displays of brute strength and burgeoning testosterone. There were unremitting splash-a-thons, armpit-farting contests, cannonballs, chicken fights, "melvins."
There were bathing suit bubble bombs bursting on the water, and suddenly, out of nowhere, there was Bobby. Eighteen-year-old Bobby, with his eighteen-year-old body. All went quiet as he did a handspring off the aluminum ladder into their midst, his manly legs deftly breaking the surface.

Billy grew sly in the presence of his older brother. Strategically, he exploited the intrusion.

"Show them how you make the vacuum hose suck your dick," Billy smirked as he reached for the attachment. Bobby looked around at the anxious boys' faces.

With a snarl, he retorted, "They'll tell their mothers."

Without any hesitation the subdued assemblage chimed, "NO WE WON'T! DO IT!"

Billy attached the vacuum hose to the filter, undid the skimmer nozzle from the free end, and pushed it toward his brother with contempt. He seemed to forget that it was his idea. The circle of boys moved in closer as Bobby pulled the waistband of his trunks below his scrotum and plunged his swelling penis up the hose. The suction sound was audible, a long screeching gurgle that sent the boys into paroxysms of laughter. Soon everyone was fighting for a chance to fuck the hose. Pandemonium had broken out in the suburbs, until suppertime called a temporary draw.

Tony was the first to hit the street that evening. Tony was an exceptional boy for his age; premature in just about every way. He shaved nearly every day. He had lost both his parents by the time he was ten, and was living with Jenny, his older, married sister. He was spinning bottles and making out fairly frequently by the time he reached ninth grade. Normal experimentation. But some nights, he prowled for something else to get into.

More and more, it would be some strange man's car, where Tony performed a variety of very precocious services to the wonder and surprise of anonymous johns. He had discovered a netherworld of country roads and rest stops where Long Island men of a certain predisposition ravenously hunted for game. Tony was game: chicken in camouflage, with a Marlon Brando slouch and five o'clock shadow. To add fuel to the fire, his older cousin, Andy, a hairdresser and amateur dancer, had recently purchased the last available house in the development. Andy tutored Tony with a cache of porn films.

Among his peers at school it was a different matter. Tony was desperate to fit in, so he threw himself into the dating scene, asking different girls to go steady several times a month. He spent a fortune on ankle bracelets.

(*He sings wildly—the Beatles' "I'm Down."*)
YOU TELL LIES THINKIN' I CAN'T SEE
YOU CAN'T HIDE 'CAUSE YOU'RE LAUGHIN' AT ME
I'M DOWN…

(He stops himself abruptly.)

At eight o'clock that evening all the boys reconvened at Peter and Skippy DaVinci's house. Their parents were in the city seeing Dionne Warwick at the Copacabana.

Anarchy was in the air that night, and boys who were normally well-behaved, obedient types found themselves in the grip of a lawless frenzy. It was fun, for example, for Catholic Jack Powers to show off when he discovered Mr. DaVinci's antique scabbard by plunging its blade through Mrs. DaVinci's plastic slipcovers. It was also fun for Billy to chug-a-lug Johnnie Walker Black when he uncovered it behind the wet bar. But what was most fun was turning up the volume on Peter's latest 45, "Wild Thing" by the Troggs.

Billy was the first one to feel no pain, so naturally he kicked off the proceedings.

(He sings.)
WILD THING, I THINK I LOVE YOU
BUT I WANT TO KNOW FOR SURE
COME ON, HOLD ME TIGHT
I LOVE YOU

The boys, who had arranged themselves about the impeccably appointed den with the chartreuse shag carpet, began clapping and catcalling. Skippy, the youngest, whistled through his fingers from the ottoman while Bobby posed insouciantly on a barstool perch, imperturbable in his seniority. Catholic Jack Powers ground his acned behind back and forth in his blue jeans, while Peter and Tony sat galvanized at either end of the couch.

(*He sings.*)

WILD THING

SHAKE IT SHAKE IT, WILD THING

Before them all, Billy gyrated in his cut-off chinos and boat-necked shirt. His eyes rolled back into his head, his hands jiggled, and he hopped from foot to foot as an Iroquois medicine man might to drive the fever out of a sick man.

He began to rub himself suggestively from head to foot. He pulled his glasses off and undid the laces of his sneakers. By the time he peeled his shirt over his sweat-drenched hair, his teenaged torso glistened with rivulets. Teasingly, he cracked his shirt like a whip, spun it like a lariat. Then he wiped his chest with it and flung it over Skippy. "Pop!" went the snap at his waistband and the music didn't matter anymore.

"TAKE IT OFF…ALL THE WAY!" erupted from the spectators, urgent and ferocious. No one was laughing now. They were fiercely determined to see all of Billy Crane exposed. Tony kept one eye discreetly trained on Bobby.

With a series of suggestive thrusts, Billy let his shorts drop, revealing pee-stained briefs. He kept on thrusting. Turning toward the glass doors, he yanked the fiberglass drapes open and pressed himself against the full-length windows.

He forgot about the others then and kissed his own reflection, which glowed amber against the blue backyard floodlights. He slid his torso up and down. He trembled. With one abrupt move he reached behind with both hands and tore his BVDs off his ass.

Jack began to clap again. "MORE! MORE!"

And slowly, Billy turned toward the room, fully naked, tumescent. "HE ISN'T CIRCUMCISED!" Skippy hollered.

Now Billy's face was fearsome as he danced and humped and shook. He flopped his penis up and down, banged it on his thighs—left-right, left-right. He wagged it. He reached out to the glass coffee table, grabbed the Johnnie Walker, raised it to his lips and swallowed hard. He let it spill out of his mouth until it ran down past his belly, drenching his swollen genitals.

"STOP IT!" Peter screamed. "YOU'RE GONNA WRECK THE CARPET!" His protests were in vain. The spell could not be broken.

Suddenly, the sound of the automatic garage door rumbled through the house as Eleanor and Vince DaVinci pulled into the driveway in their long white Pontiac Bonneville.

(*Breathlessly, he moves left and crouches behind the trunk.*)
Fifteen minutes later, Bobby and Billy Crane and Tony huddled behind Mr. Crane's toolshed, giddy and breathless from their perilous escape. Billy was drunk and naked.

"Did you see Jack scale the fence? I think he's got my glasses!" Billy squealed, doubling in half.

"Shut up, you stupid asshole," Bobby whispered fiercely.

"We're in deep shit right now," said Tony.
(*As Bobby.*)
"Man, Peter and Skippy better keep their mouths shut."
(*As Billy.*)
"They're screwed! God, I'm horny."

A look passed between Tony and Bobby.
(*As Tony.*)

"You wanna take a walk with me and see if we can find the other guys?"

(*As Bobby.*)

"Sure. Go to bed, Billy. Don't let Dad see your ass."

Billy stumbled blindly toward their house.

On their tour of the neighborhood, Tony and Bobby didn't talk much, but they sensed a certain kinship. Tony'd heard a lot about Bobby from Billy, while Bobby knew nothing about him. He assumed Tony was at least seventeen. He looked so rugged with his beard shadow and thick, brown, wavy hair.

"You Italian?" he asked.

"Yep," Tony answered.

"I'm half German, half Irish."

"Yeah, I know." They scanned the night. There was no one to be found. The others were all home now. It was almost one a.m. Then, boldly, Tony said,

"You circumsized?"

(*As Bobby.*)

"Yeah. You were in the pool today. You?"

(*As Tony.*)

"Yeah. Wanna see?"

(*As Bobby.*)

"Right here? I dare ya."

(*As Tony.*)

"No. Come over to my place. Everyone's asleep. It's dark on the side of the house."

They kept walking side by side, barely looking at each other. Their steps quickened involuntarily as they rounded Tony's corner and approached his dark house in silence. Tony led them to the garage side. Once there, behind some junipers, he stopped and turned on Bobby.

"You first," baited Bobby. "It was your idea."

(*As Tony.*)

"Uh-uh. You go first."

"Alright," Bobby acquiesced proudly. He unclipped his belt and pulled his pants open. Without a second thought, so did Tony. They both were hard and trembling. They both were circumsized, of equal length, though Bobby's was thicker. They stared for a few seconds, then Bobby started covering up.

(*As Tony.*)

"Wait. Put your hand on mine."

(*As Bobby.*)

"No way."

(*As Tony.*)

"Come on. I won't tell anyone."

(*As Bobby.*)

"You first."

And Tony reached out. His head was full of "What if he…?" and "Maybe I'm…?" and "Don't be first." But what he wanted didn't have a thing to do with thinking. His hand stroked Bobby's penis with a gentle, warm caress.

Bobby drew his breath in through his teeth. He had never been touched by anyone except once, in a drunken stupor, when he forced himself on Billy. He moaned. Tony kept his hand there for six or seven seconds, then released it.

"Okay, you," he proferred, and Bobby complied. He gripped Tony's penis with the tightest grip possible.

"Not so hard!" Tony hissed. Bobby slackened. He moved his fist up and down a bit. Tony closed his eyes. Bobby moved beside him and kept jerking.

Each of them was panting now, Bobby's face close to Tony's neck. A breeze came up, but Bobby's hot breath in his ear was the only air Tony was aware of.

Abruptly, Bobby pulled away. "That's enough," he ordered.

"Wait!" Dropping to his knees, he guided Bobby in front of him and put his penis in his mouth. "Now you," he said, standing up again. Bobby hesitated, and then he did the same. "Don't use your teeth!" Tony winced.

Bobby's rough, inexperienced mouth enveloped him briefly, then he stood up, spitting. "Jerk me off," he whispered.

The two boys moved in closely. Standing face to face, their hands pumping quickly, they ejaculated on the ground between them in under a minute, Bobby first, then Tony, even more profusely.

That was it. Tony said, "See ya." Bobby grunted and went home. They didn't see each other again 'til *Rubber Soul* Christmas, when

Bobby came home on leave from basic training. That August he had joined the Marines.

> (*Back at the upstage end of the trunk, he opens it again and The Beatles' "Bad Boy" plays. He pulls items from the trunk: an album cover, a yearbook. Finally, he takes three white roses out and dances like a wild boy with the flowers, smashing them and scattering their petals stage left. As the song fades, he closes the trunk and sits on it.*)

On December 28th, 1965, Tony turned fifteen. The next day, his family drove up to Massachusetts to spend New Year's week with in-laws. For the first time in his life, Tony was left alone in the house with six days and nights to himself. His cousin Andy was right up the block if he needed anything. (*Crossing stage right.*) Andy had a big heart and always took a special interest in the adventures of his precocious cousin. He wasn't the brightest counselor Tony'd ever had. In fact, when he heard that Jenny and her husband were heading up to New England he startled Tony by asking, "How far is Boston from Massachusetts?"

On Sunday afternoon Tony dropped in on him hoping to watch a few fuck films, but Andy was entertaining several "show biz" friends from Manhattan, one of whom had been a principal dancer in "I Can Get It For You Wholesale" with Barbara Streisand. His pants were especially tight. Tony beat a hasty retreat.

(He sings the Beatles' "Norwegian Wood.")

SHE ASKED ME TO STAY AND SHE TOLD ME TO SIT ANYWHERE

SO I LOOKED AROUND AND I NOTICED THERE WASN'T A CHAIR…

Feverish over the Beatles' latest release, *Rubber Soul*, Billy called often.

When Tony returned from Andy's that Sunday, the phone was ringing.

(As Billy, in the stage right chair.)

"I think 'You Won't See Me' is my favorite."

(As Tony.)

"Oh, come on. 'Norwegian Wood' is fantastic."

(As Billy.)

"Bobby says it sounds like shit. Yesterday he yanked the needle off and scratched it."

(As Tony.)

"When's he going back?"

(As Billy.)

"Not until January 7th."

(As Tony.)

"Does he wear a uniform?"

Billy hesitated before answering. Tony could hear him take a long drag on a cigarette.

(*As Billy.*)

"Yeah, 'dress blues,' but he's still a slob."

When Tony got off the phone he changed his shirt and walked over to the Cranes' house.

One of the smaller Crane kids was playing with a Tonka truck on the porch, in filthy underwear. It was thirty-four degrees outside. The kid looked blue.

Billy answered the bell.

(*As Billy.*)

"Ricky! Get inside, you asshole." He grabbed his little brother by the hair and pulled him in as he held the door for Tony. The place stank of cat spray.

"Come on upstairs. I just finished tracing the album cover. I think it looks fantastic."

Billy shared a room with Bobby, whose bed, despite Billy's indication to the contrary, was made Marine-style now; hospital

corners, army-issued blanket. A trunk with his initials, "R.C.",
embossed on it stood at its foot. Above it, one poster: Raquel Welch.

(*As Tony.*)

"Where's your brother?"

(*As Billy.*)

"Who cares. Out." He turned his bedside lamp to shine on the wall
where *Rubber Soul* was freshly drawn. Surrounding it were tracings
of each Beatles album, colored in with crayon. "Behold, the second
coming."

"Cool," said Tony. He knelt on the bed to get a closer look and a cat
hissed, scrambling out from under. "This one's the best."

(*As Billy.*)

"It was easier than *Beatles '65.*"

(*As Tony.*)

"Yeah. Their faces are bigger. That really looks like John."

Billy felt great about that. He liked drawing John. He always thought
Tony looked like John.

(*As Billy.*)

"So how's the house by yourself?"

(*As Tony.*)

"It's great. I get to turn the heat way up and walk around naked. Last night I got up at three o'clock in the morning and listened to the radio."

(*As Billy.*)

"Cool."

(*He takes a drag on an imaginary cigarette.*)

"Cool."

(*As Tony.*)

"New Year's Eve they're gonna play the Top 100 of the year. You should come over. My sister's got a drawerful of sample cigarettes."

(*As Billy.*)

"I have to babysit."

(*As Tony.*)

"That's shitty."

(*As Billy.*)

"Yeah."

(*As Tony.*)

"Why can't Bobby babysit?"

(*As Billy.*)

"I don't know, ask him."

Tony didn't say he would, but that's what he was thinking. They sat in silence, staring at the wall.

(*Transition sound.*)

New Year's Eve day it snowed. A lot. Some people shoveled early, before the storm let up. The rumbling of the DaVincis' El Toro snowblower brought Tony out of the house around three. He walked up to the main road and stuck his thumb out to a few slow-moving vehicles, but no one stopped. He gave up after fifteen minutes or so. Alone and full of longing, he turned toward home. The development was aglow beneath a heavy white cover of snow, and he felt a delicious melancholia set in; a deep, hollow feeling which he savored as only a young man can.

He was enthralled with himself. With nature. It made him feel part of something bigger. Like a tree, or a dog…a figment from Jack London. Exquisitely lonely.

Tramping back, about halfway home, he saw an overbundled figure with a shovel in one hand emerge from the Cranes' house. It was Bobby.

Bobby was a poor shoveler. Haphazard and distracted. He did what he had to do, no more. It was the first time Tony'd seen him since he returned from basic training.

(*He howls.*)

"How ya doin'?" he called out from the middle of the snowbound street. Bobby stopped and looked at him.

(*As Bobby.*)

"Real good. How're you?" His voice was different; deeper, slightly warmer. He even smiled a little without smirking.

(*As Tony.*)

"Good. I'm real good. How're the Marines?"

The old shadow passed over Bobby's face. "They're… something," he smirked, and chipped at some deep ice.

(*As Tony.*)

"You look different."

(*As Bobby.*)

"Yeah? You don't." Bobby dropped his shovel and tramped over. "It's fucking freezing here."

(*As Tony.*)

"Where you stationed?"

(*As Bobby.*)

 "Atlanta, Georgia now, but I'll be moved to D.C. next month." (*He looks pissed.*)

(*As Tony.*)

"You should come over later. I've got the whole house to myself."

(*As Bobby.*)

"Yeah?" (*He spits.*) "Where's your sister?"

(*As Tony.*)

"Massachusetts. There's a lot of alcohol my brother-in-law got for Christmas from his real estate office and…uh…I really want to hear what the Marines are like in case I'm drafted or something, right? Come over."

(*As Bobby.*)

"Maybe…what time?"

(*As Tony.*)

"I don't care, like nine o'clock?"

(*As Bobby.*)

"Maybe."

Tony played it very cool and walked away. "Okay. See ya," and in afterthought he called over his shoulder, "Happy New Year!"

"You, too!" Bobby packed a quick snowball and threw it deliberately off target.

Tony turned just as the snowball exploded against a telephone pole. Smiling, walking backward, he flipped Bobby the finger. Then he ran.

(*He runs in place.*)

When he got back home he turned the radio up loud, ate canned soup, and took the hottest bath he could stand. The countdown was on: number thirty-seven, "This Diamond Ring" by Gary Lewis and the Playboys. He shaved and splashed himself with Hai Karate.

(*The intro to the Beatles' "Michelle" plays.*)

At ten minutes to nine the doorbell rang. Being early was a good sign. Tony answered the door barefoot, in a white t-shirt and chinos.

(*As Tony.*)

"Come on in. Just throw your stuff down anywhere." Bobby entered gruffly. "You want potato chips?"

(*As Bobby.*)

"What's to drink?"

(*As Tony.*)

"You choose."

Bobby opened his parka and threw it over the stairway railing. He pulled his woolen cap off revealing for the first time a regulation buzz-cut.

"Wow, short," admired Tony as he led him to the dining room. "How 'bout…Johnnie Walker?"

(*He raises his eyebrows up and down, Groucho-style.*)

(*As Bobby.*)

"Nah. Vodka and orange juice…if you have it."

(*As Tony.*)

"Yeah, I do. The glasses are up above. Help yourself. I'll get the Tropicana."

Bobby didn't help himself. He waited for Tony to come back with the juice.

(*As Bobby, snorting.*)

"What's that smell?"

(*As Tony.*)

"Hai Karate aftershave. I got it for Christmas."

(*He mixes two drinks.*)

"Let's go into the den. The countdown is on. They're up to number nineteen."

(*He crosses to the stage right chair.*)

They lounged for awhile on the bamboo set, listening, drinking, eating potato chips. Bobby was fidgety. Finally, Tony turned the radio off and began.

(*As Tony.*)

"So what's it like?"

(*As Bobby.*)

"It's tough. They make you do stuff all the time. The sergeant's a big asshole, but I'm getting in good shape. You wouldn't like it."

(*As Tony.*)

"Yeah, why not?"

Bobby blushed, looking almost handsome beside the pink den lamp.

(*As Bobby.*)

"I don't know. I wouldn't recommend going in right now. They're sending guys over to Vietnam and it's pretty fucked up there. What are you, seventeen?"

(*As Tony.*)

"Fifteen."

(*As Bobby.*)

"Really? You look a lot older."

(*As Tony.*)

"Yeah, I always have. A girl at the dentist's office last week asked me what college I go to. She couldn't believe I'm fifteen. I like it."

(*As Bobby.*)

"Yeah. You're mature."

Silence. Another round of drinks. The heat in the house was up very high.

The windows steamed. Bobby unbuttoned his shirt and pulled his shirttails out over his fatigue pants. An involuntary moan rumbled in Tony's throat.

(*As Tony.*)

"You get to sleep with girls on the base?"

(*As Bobby.*)

"Yeah, right. On the base? No way. It's really strict. There's a lot of talk and, ya know, sometimes weekends…I don't know. Atlanta's funny. I don't like the South."

(*As Tony.*)

"Is it…prejudiced?"

(*As Bobby.*)

"Yeah…I don't know. No…I guess. There's prostitutes and stuff. It's a big city."

He looked down into his glass. "This shit's really strong."

Tony sensed Bobby's discomfort and it made him sad. They caught each other's eyes for a half beat too long.

Bobby shifted. "Well, I guess I should go."

(*As Tony.*)

"No, wait a second. Let's…let's go upstairs."

(*As Bobby.*)

"What, to the bedroom?"

(*As Tony.*)

"My sister's got a big bed. Come on."

Bobby took a good long look at Tony, who now stood at the couch with his hands plunged in his pockets expectantly. "Alright," he said. When he stood up his stiff penis pushed his shirt front out.

Tony led him upstairs taking two steps at a time. They moved down the darkened hallway quickly. Tony had taken special care to light the master bedroom dimly. He'd even turned the covers down just so. His sister's bed was huge.

They stood on either side of it. They took their own clothes off, watching each other all the while. For the first time they saw each other completely naked. Then they got on the bed, but didn't touch. There was still too much at stake in this. Neither could begin without a promise from the other to reciprocate. Tony smelled too sweet and Bobby too musky. Tony suggested they shower together, but Bobby thought that would be queer, so they forewent the shower. Taking careful turns…repeating—hands, lips, mouth—like last summer. At one point, deep in pleasure, Tony had Bobby lie on top of him and place his penis in between his legs. Bobby's hot chest pressed down, and once again the sound of his breath filled Tony's ear. Then, face to face, they came.

Tony tried to kiss him but Bobby wouldn't have it, which made Tony self-conscious and a little mad. Separated, they cleaned themselves off with bath towels.

"So you're here for how much longer?" Tony asked once they were back downstairs and Bobby was putting on his parka.

(*As Bobby.*)

"'Til the seventh, but I've got a lot to do."

(*As Tony.*)

"Okay, well, it was good seeing you."

(*As Bobby.*)

"You too." With a sudden clumsy impulse he kissed Tony on the mouth. "Happy New Year."

(*As Tony.*)

"It isn't midnight yet."

(*As Bobby.*)

"Close enough," and he stepped out the door, spitting in the snow.

Tony watched him disappear down the long front path of his house. He was glad he was gone. He might still catch the top ten of the countdown. Number seven was playing: "Michelle."

(*The sound of a slow, lush song comes up. He crosses right to the chair, sits, and pulls a long, red fabric out from behind the chair. He slides it tenderly over his face until he reaches the end of it, then he rises and begins to twirl, finally throwing it down abruptly, and the music cuts out. He crosses center.*)

A year and a half later, in the spring of '67, just before the "Summer of Love," Tony was arbitrarily jumped and beaten unconsious by a local gang. Eight teeth cracked. It changed him profoundly. He stopped confiding in Billy Crane altogether then. He couldn't afford to maintain vulnerable allies. Their Beatles thing fell by the wayside. When he did go out with kids his own age, they roamed the streets after dark as outlaws; smoking, sniffing glue, breaking into parked cars. Their leader was John Fichetti, a.k.a. "Fork."

Like Tony, Fork was physically precocious, but he improved on nature's gifts with his own regimen: lifting weights, sculpting himself into a titan at a time when teenaged titans were rare. He was the toughest streetfighter Tony'd ever seen.

Accordingly, he inducted a scrappy collection of insurgents as his sidekicks.

They were losers and fuck-ups mostly, but they gathered loyally around their leader, who in turn guaranteed absolute security. Constituting a small battalion of latter-day gladiatiors—fearless troublemakers and their battered consigliere, Tony—together, they laid siege to Central High.

Tony was suspended for truancy in October of his junior year. He had been skipping classes with Fork's crowd when his sister spotted him outside Miano's Pizzeria. She and her husband decided to keep him out of school indefinitely.

(*As his sister, Jenny.*)

"You want to be out, you're out. Discussion closed."

He moped about sullenly. There were a certain number of chores he was required to do around the house. His phone privileges were severely restricted. But he did manage to see Fork and the boys when his family was out shopping one Thursday on a long hunt for new appliances. Halloween week.

(*He sings the Beatles' "Strawberry Fields" as he crouches center.*)

LET ME TAKE YOU DOWN CAUSE I'M GOING TO…

The gang met in a wooded area adjacent to the development. It was a cloudy afternoon, and somehow they stumbled across a stack of pornographic "chapbooks" near a rotting woodpile. Flimsy pamphlets without pictures, just lurid, detailed accounts. Most were heterosexual. Two were not.

The boys sat in a circle as freckle-faced Hurley, a dimwitted Tom Sawyer-type with a sadistic streak, scratched his balls and recited certain homo passages with relish. The boys would fake throwing up when they heard chapter titles like "Texan's Butt Smells Like Baklava," or "The Cop Showed Me His Pistol."

Tony did his best to go along, but he payed close attention to what was happening to Fork during Hurley's sardonic recitation. He could see a ramrod stiffness gradually rise up Fork's spine. He recognized that animal belligerance. He'd seen him in action, the pounding piston fists. His own secret life felt mountainous. Unhideable. A limp wrist, a lisp, a swish…

(*As Tony.*)

"I know the fag who prob'ly stashed those books here," he blurted. Quietly, all eyes turned toward him.

(*As Fork.*)

"Who is it, T.? Who's the fag and how do you know him?" Fork inquired. "Is it your cousin?"

(*As Tony.*)

"No, it's not my cousin. You remember Bobby, Billy Crane's older brother? The bozo who joined the Marines after high school? He lives right here in my development. They kicked him out of the Marines. He's a homo."

(*As Hurley.*)

"How do you know?" Hurley shot at him. "Did you fuck him?"

(*As Tony.*)

"No, I didn't fuck him. He fucks his brother." The group howled. It was perfectly plausible to imagine Billy Crane compromised. Billy Crane, the art teacher's brown-nose? Billy Crane, whose First-Prize Poster for Fire Prevention Week was prominently displayed in the Art Department's showcase? *That* Billy Crane?!

The joke relieved Tony of any incriminating pressure for the moment. He stood up casually to head back home.

(*As Fork.*)

"Wait a minute, T. Wait a minute. You said Bobby Crane's around?" said Fork.

(*As Tony.*)

"I don't know. I think so. Why?"

(*As Fork.*)

"Get him over your house tonight. We'll have a party."

(*As Tony.*)

"No, Fork. No. I'm up shit's creek as it is."

(*As Fork.*)

"Come on, we'll just play around. No trouble. We'll just give him a little 'fag test' and send him home."

(*As Hurley.*)

"What's a 'fag test'?" Hurley asked, suspiciously.

(*As Fork, rising.*)

"You get him to look at his fingernails to see if they're clean or dirty. If he bends them this way…"

71

(*The Narrator turns his knuckles in, palms up.*)

"…then he's one of us. If he turns them up like this…"

(*He splays his fingers wide, palms down.*)

"…he's a fag."

(*An ominous sound.*)

Tony's horror could barely be disguised. Gamely, he faked amusement while his knees locked beneath him like vises.

Fork pressed on. "Okay, Tony, here's the deal. Nine o'clock he's at your house.

"We'll convene before then by the high-tension wires. If your bedroom light is *out* we'll meet you on the side of your garage. With 'fruitsy.' If your bedroom light is *on*, we'll talk tomorrow. But just make sure he's there, okay?"

Fork was so charming, so cavalier, but Tony knew better. He knew that any plan made by Fork had to be respected, and to fail to produce Bobby would not just blemish his allegiance, but…

(*He minces upstage to Japanese music.*)

Walking back alone up the middle of the development, Tony felt disembodied.

It was nearly dark. The low and heavy cloud covering had forced an early twilight. His stomach churned. He wanted nothing more then than to leave Long Island forever. He wanted to continue up to the main road and stick his thumb out until a series of cars and trucks lifted him out of the mess he was in and carried him out west, to California. He wanted his parents back, alive, involved, to escort him off to boarding school or commit him to the asylum. Even shock therapy didn't seem preposterous.

"Fucking Bobby Crane. Fucking Bobby Crane." Like a battle hymn that phrase drummed in his brain. He turned up the Crane's driveway, resolvedly.

Billy answered the door. It was about 6:15. He was eating corn chips.

(*As Billy.*)

"Hi. Haven't seen you in ages. What's up? You look pissed."

(*As Tony.*)

"I'm not. Is Bobby home?"

(*As Billy.*)

"Yeah, why? You know someone who cares? Have you seen him?"

(*As Billy, he calls upstairs.*)

"Baaah-BEE!" he yodelled up the staircase.

"WHAT?" came back down with a thud.

(*As Billy.*)

"Tony's here to see you." (*He turns to address Tony.*) "You wanna come in?"

    (*As Tony.*)

"No, I'd better not."

Billy slammed the screen and vanished. Tony let his breath out in a long sigh and realized he'd been holding it for some time. The sequence of events that had led him here flooded back into his brain. "Fucking Bobby Crane."

And the screen door opened and there he was.

He was fuller, probably eighteen or twenty pounds heavier and most of that in his gut. His skin was pale and greyish, his eyes looked dark and hurt. His hair was unkempt and greasy in spots. He hadn't shaved. He was in flannel pajama pants, a torn V-neck t-shirt and dirty white socks. He looked like his father. And he smelled. Beer smell. Tony held his breath again.

"How you doin'?" he said, and wished he hadn't. It was obvious.

Bobby didn't look at him. "Awright."

    (*As Tony.*)

"When d'ja get back?"

    (*As Bobby.*)

"'Bout a month ago."

(*As Tony.*)

"You uh…you feel like gettin' together later?"

Now Bobby looked at him. "For what?"

(*As Tony.*)

"I don't know…just to talk."

Bobby belched and smirked. It took all Tony had in him not to turn away. He fixed his stare on Bobby. Finally, Bobby said, "Nine o'clock okay?"

(*As Tony.*)

"No. Make it eight thirty. I'm on curfew these days. I'll meet you on the side of my house."

Bobby tried to smile but it didn't hold. When Tony saw the attempt it made his chest constrict. "See you then," he said and cut across the lawn.

When he turned the corner of his block he saw his sister's car in the driveway alongside someone's V.W. hatchback. It was just after dark. Jack-o'-lanterns glowed.

He braced himself, but when he walked in he was greeted with a jovial reception. His uncle had shown up with cake, there was a new, double-doored refrigerator with an ice-making device hooked up.

Everyone was cheerful and loud, the kids were hunting for bad guys in the den, and "Fiddler on the Roof" was halfway through the sacking of the shtetl. Even his beleaguered sister, Jenny, after giving him the evil eye as he entered the room, loosened up enough by dinner time to kiss him on the cheek. He was so grateful to be included again, he helped set the table and clear the plates. Sometime after eight, he was in the kitchen double-bagging trash, laughing with and among the adults, when the front bell rang. All bustling ceased.

"Who the hell is that now?" his brother-in-law, Jim, griped.

"Uncle Tony!" his little niece called from the living room, "It's a man called Bobby."

"I'll get it," said Tony, rushing forward with the trash in his hand. Reaching the door, he said, "You're early."

　　(*As Bobby.*)
"Yeah. You got company?"

　　(*As Tony.*)
"It's my uncle. Come on, I've got to dump this." He slipped out past the curious kids. Bobby followed him.

　　(*As Bobby.*)
"This okay?"

(*As Tony.*)

"Yeah, it's just company. Come on…"

They headed around the garage side of the house. Bobby had put himself together some since Tony saw him earlier. Washed and shaved and combed.

He had on a nice shirt—too small—and a clean pair of fatigue pants. He still looked pale, and the dark circles under his eyes made him look ghoulish in the blue-green streetlamp light. The extra weight made him look shorter. His scent was overpoweringly sweet.

As they rounded the back corner of the house where the garbage cans were hidden, Tony flinched. "What cologne are you wearing?"

(*As Bobby.*)

"'Jade East.'

(*A chord of Japanese music plays.*)

"I used too much, I think."

(*As Tony.*)

"Yeah, it's really strong." Tony dropped the trash in a can. Then he thought of something. "Hold it a second." He ran a few paces away from the side wall of the house and looked up over the garage. The light in his room was lit. "Shit," he said to himself, then ran past Bobby announcing, "I'll be right back."

He entered the house quickly, ran up the stairs and down the hall to his bedroom where two of the kids were jumping on his bed. He shooed them out, shut the light and closed the door behind him.

"There's a monster in my closet. Don't go in there," he chided as he passed the kids on the staircase. They squealed and took off for the den.

Bobby was back at the side of the house, leaning against it. Opposite, the junipers that had sheltered their first encounter were much taller now. There were a few toys scattered underneath them, including a Big Wheels.

> (*He moves upstage and slowly crosses along the wall, left to right.*
>
> (*As Tony.*)

"What's goin' on?"

> (*As Bobby.*)

"Nothin'. Just waiting."

> (*As Tony.*)

"Why'd ya get kicked out?"

> (*As Bobby.*)

"I fucked up."

> (*As Tony.*)

"Was it sex?"

(*As Bobby, he snorts.*)

"No, it wasn't. Let's get goin'."

(*As Tony.*)

"I can't leave."

(*As Bobby.*)

"I don't mean leave. Let's go over there."

(*Nothing happens. He turns his head toward Tony.*)

"Well?"

(*As Tony.*)

"I don't wanna. Not yet."

(*As Bobby, he leans in close.*)

"Come on. I'll kiss you this time."

(*The sound of a stick cracking. They separate.*)

"Who's that?" Tony whispered to the darkness.

(*As Fork.*)

"Hey, Tony. What's going ooon?" Fork cooed as he emerged from the black back yard. Behind him were his henchmen.

(*As Tony.*)

"Nothin', nothing's going on. Bobby was just telling me about Washington, D.C."

"Really? D.C.?" said Hurley, slithering into view. The gang was within ten feet of where the couple stood and they were forming a semi-circle. Bobby was silent.

"I didn't know they let *fags* in D.C.," Hurley continued. Bobby's body stiffened.

(*As Tony.*)

"Shut up, Hurley. Shut up."

Hurley laughed. (*He laughs, squealingly.*) "I guess that's what D.C. stands for: 'Dick Crazed.'"

(*As Bobby, looks at Tony.*)

"What is this?"

(*As Tony.*)

"They're fucked up." (*To the gang.*) "Just fuck off, guys. Fuck off."

Then, just what Tony didn't want to happen was happening. Fork moved forward quickly. With a jolt, his hands grabbed Bobby's shirt front so fast they were practically invisible, and before Tony could even think, Bobby was flipped over and backward through the air. He landed awkwardly, tripping on the Big Wheels, and toppled lopsidedly into the junipers, his left hand twisting painfully behind him. He tried to spring up again before the circle closed in on him, but Fork was on him right away, pounding. Bobby got one punch in sidehanded at Fork's ear, which is when Hurley started kicking.

(*He crosses menacingly down center, turns upstage, and enacts a terrifying ritual bashing.*)

"MOTHERFUCKIN' FAIRY! FAGGOT! FRUIT! COCKSUCKER! FAG FAG FAG!"

(*He moves back upstage, and leans against the wall.*)

Time stopped. For Tony, it felt like the time he fell off the top of a ten foot ladder: slow motion and the certainty of pain. He clung to the side of the house, immobile. There were just sounds; thuds, tearing, breathing, grunts. It was all over in under thirty seconds.

(*A sound like a bell rings out.*)

The gang backed off loosely. Bobby was struggling up to his feet, his hands groping for the buttons that had been torn from his shirt. There was a lot of blood around his mouth and one eye was already swelling shut. He was disoriented, sluggishly trying to extricate himself from the juniper bushes.

Tony remained frozen to his spot, rocking slightly. Fork came up to him panting, with a half smile. A small trickle of blood ran from his ear. "Fuck made my ear bleed." He wiped it with the back of his hand and patted Tony's shoulder. "Let us know if he fucks with you again."

They started moving off. "Bye, Mary," Hurley minced past Bobby menacingly. "Kiss a sailor for me next time you're in D.C. Fucking faggot."

When they'd gone, Tony didn't move. He didn't offer to help or try to say anything. Bobby got himself together slowly. He didn't look at Tony. He said nothing to him. He walked around the house and down the driveway.

The air was still.

("Wild is the Wind"—the Johnny Mathis version—fades up.

He crosses downstage left and sits on the trunk as he speaks.)
After a few minutes, muffled laughter from within penetrated the wall outside, and Tony went back into the house. The kids were gathered around the TV in the living room watching "The Outer Limits." He joined the adults in the den, where he helped his brother-in-law stoke the fire in the fireplace, above which hung a mantle full of photos.

(The music swells and fades.)
The year preceeding graduation from high school was extraordinarily eventful for Tony: '68-'69. That was the year his sister and her husband sold their house and moved back to Jim's home state, Massachusetts. Given the choice, Tony surprised everyone by deciding to finish out his senior year at Central High, and since his cousin had a spare room downstairs, he moved in with Andy. Throughout his senior year he worked as a shampoo boy in Andy's salon, scrubbing the heads of a predominantly Jewish clientele and earning sizable gratuities for his services. His strong arms and

penetrating fingers brought many women to the brink of a release they hadn't anticipated from a hairwash.

>   (*He has crossed to the stage right chair and takes his jacket off.*)

One winter evening, Andy introduced his young cousin to Mel, an assiduously moisturized beautician friend who worked down the block at *Hairistocracy*.

At twenty-nine, with a deep voice, sad brown eyes, and the pungent scent of Canoe, Mel's clientele considered him an "eligible bachelor." Tony got to ride in his car. Soon, he was picking him up after school a lot. It was Mel who taught Tony the finer arts of foreplay in the bucket seats of his yellow Karmen Ghia.
It wasn't until mid-March, Easter break, that Tony saw Bobby again.

Ironically, he was leaning on the sill of the big picture window in Andy's living room with his pants around his ankles. Mel knelt on the floor just behind him.

He had stopped by on his lunch break. Through the sheer white gauze of the curtain, Tony suddenly spotted a slim figure in a parka with a sexy girl in tow cutting through the woodlands up the street. It was Bobby. Tony came instantly.

"I wish you'd waited," said Mel from the floor as Tony pulled his pants up and wiped off the wall with a pair of dirty socks.

(*As Tony.*)

"Sorry. I was too excited. You want me to get you off?"

(*As Mel.*)

"That's alright, I've got a two o'clock perm." Mel adjusted himself as he crossed to a nearby mirror. He ran a handkerchief across his teeth. He looked past his own reflection at Tony, primping in the picture window's glass. "The problem with you is you're so damn cute and you know it. You do know it, don't you? Hey, Anthony!" Distractedly, Tony turned around.

(*As Tony.*)

"What?"

(*As Mel.*)

"Oh, forget it. I'm finished at six. Should I come back?"

(*As Tony.*)

"No. I can't tonight. I'm going to the movies with some friends."

(*As Mel.*)

"Really? What are you gonna see?"

(*As Tony.*)

"*The Graduate.*" He lied. He had already seen it twice.

Sensing this, Mel turned toward him with a big smile. "'Cu-cu-ca-choo, Mrs. Robinson.' Call me later? I'm curious to hear what you think." Tony was still preoccupied, looking out the window, so Mel took his cue to depart.

As soon as he was out of sight, Tony grabbed his jacket and headed outside.

(*He grabs his jacket and puts it on as he moves center.*)
It was a gorgeous, crisp, clear day. The ground was still frozen in places. The sun was high and his nostrils pinched with the lingering shards of a winter just past. Stepping into the well-worn path he'd seen Bobby and the girl enter, he rushed forward soundlessly, hoping to catch a glimpse of them; their huddled figures entwined against a tree, their sweating, naked backs. Anything. He found himself by the woodpile where the pact to deliver Bobby to Fork had been made last year. Another lifetime. He continued on, deeper, where the path opened onto a dirt road. A car was parked there, its windows down. He crept past it, peering in. A strange man and woman were stretched out on the back seat.

"GET THE FUCK OUTTA HERE!" …and he ran 'til he reached the far end of the woods. There wasn't a trace of Bobby to be seen.

He sprinted all the way around and back up to the Cranes' house just as Mr. Crane was pulling into the driveway.

(*As Mr. Crane.*)

"Nobody's here right now. They're away for Easter week," Mr. Crane said clambering out of his V.W. van.

(*As Tony, panting heavily.*)

"Bobby, too?"

(*As Mr. Crane.*)

"Bobby won't be back 'til later." He reached for his toolbox at the side of his van.

(*As Tony.*)

"Mr. Crane…" (*He gulps for air.*) "…could you tell Bobby…Tony came by to see him? I'm staying up…at my cousin's house…the blue one…"

Mr. Crane barely grunted. He was cutting bad plugs off of secondhand extension cords. Tony felt desperate and lied again.

(*As Tony.*)

"Tell him I need to see him…about work."

(*As Mr. Crane.*)

"He's got a job. He works with me."

(*As Tony.*)

"At the *asylum*?"

(*As Mr. Crane*)

"What's wrong with that?"

(*As Tony.*)

"Nothin'. I just…tell him I'll be home all afternoon. Number thirty-seven."

(*As Mr. Crane.*)

"Yeah, I'll tell him." The discussion over, Mr. Crane turned a cold shoulder.

Tony took a few steps backward, and ran home.

For the next few hours, he made himself busy with college applications. Eventually, with his forehead pressed against his bedroom window, he found himself repeating over and over, "Come on, come on, come on, come on…

(*Singing Janis Joplin's "Piece of My Heart."*)

"…DIDN'T I MAKE YOU FEEL…?"

By 10:30 that night, he threw himself on his bed and fell asleep staring at the ceiling fan. He was dreaming that a cockroach was gnawing at his eardrum when he woke up with a start to someone knocking. It was twenty after eleven.

Instantly awake, he hurtled up the stairs. Beneath the yellow porch light stood Bobby.

(*As Tony.*)

"Oh my god, I was having this horrible dream. How long have you been out here?"

Bobby's face was blank. "Few minutes. You live here now?"
(*As Tony.*)
"Yeah, my sister moved away. You…ya' wanna come in?"

Bobby didn't respond for a moment. "My father said you wanted to talk to me about some job."
(*As Tony.*)
"Well, sorta. Your father makes me nervous. It was the only thing I could think to say. Come in."
(*As Bobby.*)
"Anybody else in there?"
(*As Tony.*)
"No. My cousin'll be out late. It's just me. Come on."

Bobby stepped into the foyer but no farther. He stood there, reserved and unyielding. He was trim again. The bones of his face stood out angularly. His hair was thinning, but he looked good. He was twenty-one years old, a maintenance man at the asylum, but to Tony, he looked like a marine again.

88

"You want some soda?" Tony asked sheepishly. Now that he had Bobby alone, he didn't know what to say. He felt like a kid before the principal. His mouth dried up.

(*As Tony.*)

"I'm gonna get some Fresca. Want some?"

(*As Bobby.*)

"I don't need anything." In the few seconds he was left alone, he remained motionless.

Tony returned with his beverage, sat on the stairs above and popped his Fresca open.

(*As Tony.*)

"You want a sip?"

(*As Bobby, bristling.*)

"Look, it's late. I gotta work tomorrow. Why did you wanna see me?"

(*As Tony, after a pause.*)

"I thought maybe you'd like to take your clothes off with me."

(*Sound of a loud crack. As Bobby, he turns to go, then turns back.*)

"You have your own room?"

(*As Tony.*)

"Yeah, it's downstairs."

(*As Bobby.*)

"Let's go." And he followed Tony down.

The room was dark. There'd been no preparation. Bobby didn't need any. He yanked down the zipper of his pants as Tony reached for the bedside lamp.

When he flipped it on and turned back he was startled to find Bobby with his penis in his hand. He hadn't taken off his jacket. He hadn't opened his belt. He wasn't about to. He was standing in the middle of the room jacking mechanically with one hand while the other remained in his back pocket.

>*(As Bobby.)*

"Come on, hurry up."

Time was slowing down again for Tony. He sat on the edge of his bed and started to take off his socks.

>*(As Bobby.)*

"Don't do that. You want this or not?" Then he started to tuck his penis back inside his pants.

>*(As Tony.)*

"Doesn't your girlfriend like to suck your cock?"

>*(As Bobby.)*

"What girlfriend?"

>*(As Tony.)*

"The girl you went into the woods with today."

(*As Bobby.*)

"I worked all day." Bobby's eyes were cold as steel. He stepped a little forward.

"Come on, blow me."

Like walking across the bottom of the ocean, Tony stood up, crossed the room, and knelt in front of Bobby. He reached up to undo his pants.

(*As Bobby.*)

"No! Just the dick, or nothing."

Tony closed his eyes and began to suck.

(*A sound chimes.*)

After Bobby left Tony remained on the floor. Barely fifteen minutes had passed since Bobby's knock first roused him. He had come inside his pants without touching himself. He stayed up very late that night, writing. Poetry. Then he filled out the draft application that was sitting on his desk. In the blank space next to the question, "Is there any reason other than sickness or disablement that you do not qualify for the armed services?", he spelled out H-O-M-O-S-E-X-U-A-L in indelible black ink.

At about 3:45 he turned his face into his pillow, exhausted. Drifting off, he heard his cousin's car pull into the driveway, two car doors open, close, a stranger's laugh, and jangling house keys. He reached up, turned off the light, and fell asleep, his pants still sticky with his semen.

(*A sound chimes.*)

In the morning he didn't shave or wash his face. He opened the refrigerator and ate. He stuffed himself. He wrote a dozen poems that day, until the sun went down behind an impenetrable bank of clouds.

(*The sound of a driving rock song comes up, and he dances furiously, disturbing the order of the set in the process. Finally, he settles.*)

In early summer 1969, Tony left Long Island for college. He found a single room garret on St. Botolph Street in Boston, moved in, and got a job as a dishwasher in a deli in nearby Copley Square. He had grown a beard and his hair was long. He kept it brushed straight back off his face, like a penitent.

Those first few weeks in Boston, he was quick to discover the "cruising grounds" around Fenway Park, where he'd spend hours offering anonymous pleasure to anyone who'd ask. Like a penitent, he didn't get much back.

On a Saturday night at the end of his second week's work, six weeks before the official start of school, Tony heard an odd news flash. The radio on the shelf above the silverware steamer where he worked began broadcasting hourly reports about a bizarre clash between police and "deviants" in Greenwich Village. Sorting through utensils, he strained to hear the newscast over the deli's clamor:

>(*He alternates the voice of a newscaster with that of his foreign boss.*)

"...OUTSIDE THE BAR CALLED STONEWALL..."

"Silverware, pronto! Silverware, pronto!"

"...AS TRANSVESTITES POURED INTO SHERIDAN SQUARE..."

"Silverware, boy, pronto pronto!"

"...THROWING ROCKS AND BEER CANS..."

"Teaspoons, give me teaspoons!"

"...CHANTING 'STONEWALL' IN THE STREETS...A NEW 'GAY' LIBERATION...JUST HOURS AFTER PAYIING RESPECTS AT JUDY GARLAND'S WAKE."

"One a.m.! Quitting time!"

When Tony stepped into the brightly lit city after work that night, a beneficent breeze, redolent of salt, was blowing off the harbor.

He started to walk. The day he packed his bags for college, Mel had come by to see him off and to recommend a club he knew in Boston. A club simply called "The 70s."

(*As Mel.*)

"It's very discreet. An older crowd. They'll eat you up."

An older crowd. Boston Brahmins? Patriots? Longshoremen? Irish cops? Professors cloaked in tweeds with dangling pipes? Beyond fatigue, his head was filled with pictures of just which breed of predator might lie in wait tonight…to "eat him up."

With the breeze at his back he headed west, in search of… Past Kenmore Square and Fenway Park, where shadows skulked through bushes, and faceless men sat smoking in parked cars. In search of… He had a general idea of where the club might be. West. "The 70s" was west.

When he reached the dark twelve-hundred block of Boylston Street, he could hear a throbbing bass rumbling half a block away and saw a large crowd assembled at the curb. Men: old, young, colorful, drab, different heights and builds. Black, white, yellow, brown, pressing toward the threshold. Above them hung a dim red sign: "The 70s." He opened up his shirt and joined the crush.

(The sound of "Baby Love" by the Supremes comes up. He listens. Author's note: Each of these recordings was chosen not only for their period authenticity but for their textural underpinnings to the narration. A director may choose different rhythmic music from the time, but the sequence MUST culminate in the Beatles' "In My Life" where designated.)

"OOO, OO-OO, BABY LOVE, MY BABY LOVE, WHY MUST WE SEPARATE, MY LOVE?"

(The Supremes segue into Aretha Franklin's "Chain of Fools.")

"CHAIN CHAIN CHAIN, CHAIN OF FOOLS."

There were mirror balls spinning, strobes strobing, sirens, whistles, smoke. A thousand different aftershaves billowed up through the scent of cigarettes and pot and perspiration. English Leather, Royal Lime, Old Spice, Mennen Skin Bracer, Aramis, Bay Rum, Brut, Aqua Velva. So this was it, the mythical land of anything goes. An ordinary novice may have felt that they had entered Hell, but for Tony, this night—this was the center of the universe.

All at once he was dancing. Bobbing bodies thrashed and dipped and shimmied all around him. He was jostled and kissed and fondled indiscriminately. One instant, hands like tentacles slid through his open shirt, the next, strange tongues burrowed through his lips and in his ears… "Stonewall." He pushed away, breathless.

He made his way to a little clearing at the far end of the room, beneath a thick glass booth that housed the DJ. Leaning against a support beam to watch the crowd and catch his breath, his heart pounded. The world was spinning off its axis. From Stonewall weekend, the next three weeks would send him into orbit; from Neil Armstrong's "giant step" to his own small steps at Woodstock, from Charlie Manson's throne of blood to…

> (*Another Motown song, "Heat Wave" by Martha and the Vandellas, comes up, and he dances.*)

Sweat poured off his face and for the first time that night he realized that he reeked of cabbage borscht.

A few feet to his left, a sloe-eyed boy with sandy hair stood stock still, gazing at the dance floor. He seemed to be alone. He was tallish and unkempt, in a plaid shirt and painter's pants, and he occassionally cast a nervous glance back at Tony that pierced through the all-pervasive smoke. Suddenly, he smiled.

There were crowsfeet around his eyes that belied the fact that he was also just eighteen. He turned away and back, smiled again. Tony barely nodded. The last thing that he wanted was another… But when the boy turned away once more, he took a closer look. He noticed that one pant leg was inadvertantly caught inside the elastic of his sock, and this, for some reason, made his heart jump. There didn't seem to be a trace of vanity in this boy. And once again, the boy glanced at Tony.

It threw him off. He felt unmoored. He had an impulse to check to see if anyone was watching. He was so accustomed to secrets. "Stonewall! Stonewall!" rose up from the assemblage like a tribal chant, building in intensity…

(*A DJ—prerecorded—is heard, cutting off the music.*)
"Gentleman and cads! May I have your attention, puh-lease!"

The room grew still as the DJ's voice boomed through a microphone. "Thank you. In honor of this weekend's watershed, and the brave sister/boys down in Greenwich Village who are standing up to the law for all of us…" An enormous cheer burst from the crowd, topped by one very strident, "Long live Judy!" "…alright, shut up, ladies! Let's see if we can get intimate with our pants on now. Couple up! It's slow-dance time. And please, never forget from whence we came."

(*A sound chimes.*)

With that, the lights lowered, and a dramatic hush descended on the room.

Tony shifted uneasily. Then a familiar guitar phrase warmly wafted down…

(*The Beatles' "In My Life" begins playing.*)

"THERE ARE PLACES I REMEMBER

ALL MY LI-IIIFE, THOUGH SOME HAVE CHANGED…"

Tony's throat caught. He closed his eyes, tilting his head back against the post.

He felt his body trembling, his chest contracting. Tears ran down his face, torrent upon torrent, breaking through. He couldn't keep them back. He couldn't stop the spasms in his shoulders from showing, or the faces in his head from flashing by. Bobby Crane, full pale lips averted, like a wheel of fortune clown. "Fucking Bobby."

Then a warm hand pressed down on his shoulder, and when he looked, that sloe-eyed boy was staring back at him. Deeply. Inquisitively. Direct. Unafraid. Not flinching or sneering, not playing cat and mouse. Simply curious and close, in a room where men could do that…publicly. Tony cleared his throat.

(*As Tony.*)

"Hi. I'm sorry. I really… This is scary." (*He reaches out a hand.*)
"I'm Tony."

(*As Tim, offering the other.*)

"I'm Tim. You think…we should dance? Is that too weird?"
Tony put one hand on the nape of Tim's neck. No one looked. He
drew him close. No one looked. He stroked his back and a sudden
sob shook his partner's body. With Tim's tearful face on his
shoulder, Tony laughed, unexpectedly. It all seemed so peculiar.

(*As Tim.*)

"What's so funny?"

(*As Tony.*)

"Your hair smells nice. Do you use Herbal Essence?"

(*As Tim, shaking his head "No."*)

"Soap-on-a-rope. I got it for graduation."
They laughed and tried dancing, stepping on each other's toes,
swaying slowly, junior high school style…

(*He begins a slow dance to the sound of the Beatles' "In My
Life," which crossfades into Annie Lenox's version of "A
Whiter Shade of Pale." As the lights crossfade, he moves to
the trunk and sits.*)

99

POST SCRIPT

Fifteen years later, after settling down with one man for the long term, Tony came back to Long Island for his cousin Andy's funeral. He stopped at Miano's Pizzeria for a quick bite before heading back to the city. It hadn't changed. Shortly after he took his seat, a small party of young people straggled in led by a shabbily dressed man who was old enough to be...

> (*A chime.*)

They took a booth.

> (*He stands.*)

Bobby didn't recognize him. His eyes never traveled beyond the circle of young faces at his table. His arm remained draped around a teenaged girl's shoulders, who blushed each time he whispered in her ear.

> (*As the music swells, he lifts the lid of the trunk, glances back to where he imagined Bobby to be, turns out, smiles. As he closes the lid, simultaneous chord of music and...lights fade to black.*)

END OF PLAY.

Author's Note:

Dedicated to Matthew Shepard, a twenty-one year old boy I never knew who lost his life in Laramie, Wyoming, and to the several thousand victims of hate crimes every year.

My humble and profound apologies.

- T. A.

III. A FRIENDSHIP BY DEFAULT

BEAUTIFIED
The Michael – Candy Dialogues

Characters:
CANDY — a beautiful woman, ages 24 through 60.
MICHAEL — her hairdresser, ages 31 through 67.
SALLY "STARFISH" — shampoo girl, 18 and ages accordingly.

Setting:
The same hair salon throughout in Framingham, Massachusetts, its name and décor changing to represent each consecutive era. Time zig-zags from now (Prologue) to October 1969, in nine scenes back and forth through the decades, ending now again (Epilogue). To be played without intermission. *Author's Note: If an intermission MUST be installed, try it between Scenes 4 and 5.*

Production History
BEAUTIFIED was first presented in two staged readings for the INKubator Series at the Skylight Theatre in the fall of 2011 starring Mary McDonnell, Jon Tenney, and Terry Walters under the direction of Bart DeLorenzo.

In 2012, *BEAUTIFIED* received its world premiere production at the Skylight Theatre starring Karen Austin, Rob Brownstein, and Joanna Strapp under the direction of Jenny Sullivan and produced by Gary Grossman. Set and lights were designed by Jeff McLaughlin, costumes by Allison Leach, and wigs by Diane Martinous. Sound design was done by Martin Carrillo. Production stage manager was Christopher Hoffman, assisted by Colin Grossman and with promotion by Judith Borne at Borne Identities.

BEAUTIFIED
Joanna Strapp (Sally), Rob Brownstein (Mike) & Karen Austin
(Candy), Skylight Theatre

Karen Austin (Candy) & Rob Brownstein (Mike), Skylight Theatre
PHOTOS: ED KRIEGER

106

Juliet: I have forgot why I did call thee back.

Romeo: Let me stand here till thou remember it.

Juliet: I shall forget, to have thee still stand there,

Remembering how I love thy company.

Romeo: And I'll still stay, to have thee still forget,

Forgetting any other home but this.

-William Shakespeare, **Romeo and Juliet**

PROLOGUE

(A spot comes up, downstage. CANDY, *a lovely woman in her "maturity," elegantly dressed, stands facing upstage. Her hair is silvery white and stylishly cut. She turns, speaks to the audience.)*

CANDY

I don't know if enough has been said about friendship between men and women. Platonic friendship. I guess there's a case to be made against it. It's not very compelling storytelling. After all, if she's not gonna fuck him and he's not gonna fuck her over, what's the hook? Mind you, this is from a woman's perspective. Oh, I know a straight man whose best friend is a lesbian. They golf together, but that's because he just can't relax with other guys. Seeing them out there on the green, matching cardigans…it's enough to make you tear up. Not me. Like everybody trained for the daily combat of these tough times, I have an aversion to maudlin claptrap with gooey centers. *(She shades her eyes and talks to the booth.)* This is where the Celine Dion music swells.

(It does. She cuts it off.)

No thanks. Too sticky and sweet. Even when the movies touch on the subject of friendship between genders, it's usually a sidebar to the real story. The conflict, the complications that drive a good plot are usually resolved by a roll in the hay or murder, and most friends don't inflict those on each other. Well, maybe the ones you know. So, you get a yarn about the good friend at the wedding or by the hospital bed or in the mall; selfless, sympathetic, and neutered. Then there was Mike.

(MIKE *enters in the shadows upstage.*)

Mike did my hair. That probably doesn't count as friendship to you, but…neutered he was not. Ideally, I'd cue a power point presentation here, but I hate those things, and this is not a T.E.D. Talk, so you'll just have to use your imaginations and take my testimony as gospel tonight. Can I get an amen in here? (*She elicits one.*) Okay! Ready? (*Shades her eyes again, and to booth.*) Ready up there? (*To us.*) Voilà! It's 1969. (*She lifts a finger, cues. And…*)

Scene 1

(Sound of "Good Morning Starshine" by Oliver swells up as lights crossfade up on a beauty parlor. Candy slips off.

It is 1969. Framingham, Massachussetts. 9:30 a.m., a Thursday in May. Offstage entrance right. Onstage reception desk up right, upon which sits a phone, reserve book, and flowers. Center stage left, a hairdresser's chair/station. Off up left, unseen sinks and hairdryers.

Standing by the reception desk, Mike, 31, owner and beautician, conducts an interview. He sports a toupee, long sideburns, with a "Continental" look: black turtleneck, slacks, and pointy Italian shoes.

SALLY "STARFISH"—17, pretty, hair a highly teased "artichoke" circa 1960s that Mike is just finishing—stands before him just to his left, nervously answering questions as he touches up her 'do.)

SALLY

…and since I was fifteen, I worked the counter at Fonducci's Pizzeria— *(She tries to turn toward the mirror over his station.)*

Can't I just see?

MIKE

Not 'til we're done. How old are you?

SALLY

How old do I have to be to work here?

MIKE

Uh…eighteen.

SALLY

I'm eighteen.

MIKE

Because I'm interested in you. I've interviewed thirteen girls already.

SALLY

Shit, really?

MIKE

No, you're the only one who answered the ad. So, what would you say you're really good at? Special skills.

SALLY

Sweeping.

MIKE

Sweeping?

SALLY

I'm a good cleaner.

MIKE

And I've got a broom!

SALLY

I love hair product stuff. Prell. And I can shop.

MIKE

YES! (*Sits on the edge of the desk.*) Talk to me about shopping, I'm a big mall man. Do they have malls here?

SALLY

There's one in Natick.

MIKE

On Long Island, when they opened Roosevelt Field in '56, it was Disneyland to me. My Father went to work for Gimbel's, so we'd shop on the way to Jones Beach. (*Remembering.*) Oh, my God, my Grandpa, who had the worst gas, in the Falcon, would always… Nevermind. More you.

SALLY

Well, I did all the ordering for (*Overpronouncing.*) Fon*du*cci's—

MIKE

(*Snaps fingers—an idea!*) FONDUE CHEESE!

SALLY

You know Fonducci's? Off Route 9? Near Ken's Steak House?

MIKE

(*Concentrating, he jots this down on a list.*) Maybe I should put out a fondue pot for the opening. Everyone's fondue-crazy these days, right?

SALLY

(*Maintaining her separate track.*) They got roaches galore.

MIKE

Who?

SALLY

Fonducci's! Their calzone's good. But the Caputi twins—the
manager's sons, Dominic and Carmine? Carmine always smells like
chow mein.

MIKE

How is that even possible in a pizza place?

SALLY

When I interviewed there he was sniffing glue. He wanted me to try
on hot pants and go-go boots that reeked of the girl they just let go. I
said, "What is this, Shindig?"

MIKE

Fascinating.

SALLY

Dominic, the cuter one, he's serving time in Waltham now. For
arson.

MIKE

Jesus, Starfish. You make me feel like an English butler. The
toughest kid I knew growing up was Bernadette Kelly who gave me a
black eye for playing with her hair.

SALLY

Dominic gave me his ankle bracelet. I had to keep it secret or
Carmine would have slaughtered him with a pizza pallet. Dagos, you
know.

(*Mike steps away for a moment, speechless.*)

Oh, I'm sorry, you Italian?

MIKE

Yep, so first lesson here in my shop is in etiquette. Under this roof,
no ethnic slurs. Everyone's equal here. You don't want to alienate a
soul, especially the boss. Got it?

SALLY

Yeah, sorry. (*Bites her lip.*) My mom says I got a potty-mouth
problem.

MIKE

You're flinty. That's a plus sometimes. (*Checks her resume.*) No
experience in a salon?

SALLY

I'm a fast learner. After Fonducci's I worked double shifts at Colonel
Sanders' so I could pay for a night course in cosmetology. I'm gonna
do that.

MIKE

Ambitious.

SALLY

Fuck yeah.

                    MIKE

Watch your language.

                    SALLY

(*Awkward pause.*) So do I got the job?

                    MIKE

Fuck yeah.

          (*They share a laugh.*)

Okay, close your eyes.

          (*He leads her to his chair and sits her in it.*)

Don't open 'til I finish spraying.

          (*He starts spraying like crazy. She slides down.*)

Starfish! Sit still!

                    SALLY

You're a-phixiating me!

                    MIKE

The word is AS-phixiating. You should have finished high school.

          (*More spraying, and she slides lower.*)

You gotta get used to fumes, girl. (*Stops.*) Okay, finito. Now you can
look.

          (*She opens her eyes and is horrified at what she sees.*)

                    SALLY

I'd never wear my hair like this.

                    MIKE

You should. It's very flattering on you, and it's groovy, baby.

                    115

Hulabaloo-zee! You've got to stay on top of trends if you're going to be in this business.

(*She sinks.*)

Come on, sit up. Let's make a shopping list for Saturday's opening…you like to shop, I love making lists.

(*He hands her notepad and pen. She writes.*)

Go to Cumberland Farms, order two cases of champagne, Korbel, but make sure it's brut, not Asti Spumante. Get crackers. Cold cuts: ham, American and Swiss cheese, sliced. No bologna. Olive loaf is okay. A good gouda—"g-o-u-d…"—or something French but not too stinky—a brick or a wheel. (*He stops. To self.*) Should I bother with fondue? (*To Sally.*) You like fondue?

(*She shakes head no.*)

Fuck fondue. What am I forgetting?

SALLY

Cake?

MIKE

Cake! I am cake. Cake is my life. Get Entenmann's coffee cake. Okay? Vamoos!

(*He urges her out of seat, gives her cash from his drawer.*)

Wait! Put paper plates and plastic utensils down—purple, to go with the decor. And cups. A big can of Chock Full o' Nuts…half-and-half…oh, and remind me to call my sister later to thank her for the flowers.

SALLY

(*About her hairdo.*) You mind if I wash this out before I go?

MIKE

Take it out for a test drive. Let it see daylight!

SALLY

It makes me look like prom night.

MIKE

Okay listen…you never say that to a stylist. You say, "I like this."
After you get home you can put a torch to it.

(*She scowls.*)

Seriously. If you're going to work on heads you'll learn to appreciate
the formality. Remember: "The customer's approval makes all the
labor worthwhile." Repeat after me…

SALLY

"The customer's approval makes all the labor worthwhile."

MIKE

Tips won't hurt, either. You can expect one percent of my share to
start. Now get going. When you're back I'll teach you how to scrub a
head.

(*She stalls, looks on the verge of tears.*)

Alright, wash it out!

SALLY

(*Running off to the sinks.*) Thank you! Call your sister!

(*Mike rolls his eyes, moves to the front desk, picks up an envelope from the stack of invitations he's had printed up, opens one, and reads.*)

MIKE

"You are invited to the grand opening of Mr. Michael's Salon Élan— (*Winces.*) Oh, shit…

SALLY (off)

WHAT?

MIKE

They spelled "Élan" wrong!

SALLY (off)

CALL YOUR SISTER!

MIKE

GO TO THE SUPERMARKET!

(*He picks up the phone, dials, as he continues to read aloud.*) "Drop by this Saturday, May 17, 1969, bring friends, have some refresh…ya-da-ya-da…fifteen percent discount coupon on any color, cut or manicure—

(*To his sister, on the phone.*)

Lana! …yeah, I got them, they're gorgeous, thank you…what? …no, no one yet, but soon I hope…nervous. Are you coming Saturday? …great, I'll put you down. Come early, okay? Eight… who? Mom and Dad, proud? You kidding, they're in *heaven*, disapproving— (*Imitating mom.*) "You should have stayed in art school!"

(*A huge crash from offstage.*)

(*Calls off.*) WHAT THE HELL WAS THAT? STARFISH!

SALLY (off)

I'LL CLEAN IT UP…

MIKE

(*Back on phone.*) I don't know if this one's going to work out. She seems a little dim-witted…that's right, Starfish. It's…a hippie thing. Her real name is Sally…yeah, the windmills of her mind…no, she dropped out…yes, I'm sure she drops that, too. Kicks it back with Boone's Farm Apple Wine… (*Laughs.*) I'll tell her…thanks! Okay, Saturday. Love you too. Love to Joe. Bye.

(*Mike heads off right to see what Sally broke.*)

Starfish, my sister says you could get a high school equivalency diploma real easy these days…by mail—

(*…and he's out of sight.*

Beat. A young woman, Candy, 24, enters right. Very conservatively dressed—the yacht or country club set, either in blazer and brass or tennis whites. Her hairdo—a pageboy—is way too old-fashioned for someone so young. She carries a Bonwit Teller shopping bag and looks around, rather disoriented.

From the stage left "supply room" Starfish re-enters, freshly shampooed, dressed in embroidered hippie garb and beaded headband, which holds back her very long, center-parted, wet hair. She's going shopping for the salon's opening party and has Mike's list in hand. She stops dead in her tracks when she sees Candy. They appraise each other.)

SALLY

(Calling back over her shoulder.) TRICIA NIXON'S HERE!

(Sally exits right, laughing. Mike enters from stage left, wiping his hands.)

MIKE

Oh, hi. You, uh…you want to…um…?

CANDY

Make an appointment? Maybe.

MIKE

(Crossing to desk, right.) I'm wide open this afternoon. We just… this is our first day.

CANDY

(Nods. Awkward pause.) My mother'd kill me if she knew I was here.

MIKE

Is your mother…?

CANDY

Dead.

MIKE

I'm sorry.

CANDY

(*She just looks at him.*) Why are *you* sorry, you didn't kill her, did you?

MIKE

Uhhh…

CANDY

Okay, now we're both sorry. Who was that girl?

MIKE

Starfish? She's my new shampoo girl.

CANDY

(*Nods, snide.*) "Starfish?" …perfect. The "Age of Aquarius."

MIKE

She calls herself "Starfish." Her name is Sally. She's just—

CANDY

Uncouth. I'd watch your register. Girls like that have no respect for hard work.

(*Mike's starting to get annoyed.*)

I'm from Newton… (*Beat.*) Where the Fig Newton is from.

MIKE

Yes?

CANDY

You're not.

MIKE

No. No, I'm from—

                            CANDY

Elsewhere.

                             MIKE

(*Interested.*) Where?

                            CANDY

I'd guess New York.

                             MIKE

Right on.

                            CANDY

The outer boroughs. Or Long Island.

                             MIKE

You're clairvoyant.

                            CANDY

Observant. I evaluate attire, I don't read minds.

                             MIKE

(*Changing subjects.*) Okay, so…how about this Saturday? Drop by,
bring friends, have some refreshments. (*Hands her an envelope.*)
There's an invitation to our offi—

                            CANDY

What about right now?

                             MIKE

(*Off guard.*) Uhm… (*Looking through appointment book.*) I really
don't know if I—

CANDY

(*Starts to leave.*) Okay, bye.

MIKE

Wait! You're just…

CANDY

You don't have anyone else, do you?

MIKE

Alright, okay, now. You'll have to wait a half hour until—

CANDY

I don't want that girl touching my head. Besides, I just shampooed it.
(*Crossing to his chair.*) Why don't I just sit here and we'll have a
chat and you can give me an honest appraisal of your working
methods and I can decide if you're the right man for the job.

> (*She puts her Bonwit Teller bag by his station, takes a clean
> styling cape off his shelf, and sits, offering the cape like a
> challenge. He takes the dare, crosses and with great flair,
> unfurls the cape and wraps it around Candy, who flinches.*)

I never use conditioner or spray on my hair and I'm very careful
about heat. No curling irons, thank you. May I see the scissors you
use?

> (*Disbelieving, he hands her a pair.*)

Those'll do.

MIKE

(*Amused, but the fuse is getting shorter.*) Are you rea—? (*He stops *himself.*)

CANDY

What? Republican? Rich? Radioactive?

MIKE

I was going to ask if you were reading anything?

CANDY

Yes, I am, as a matter of fact, thank you. Barry Goldwater's
Conscience of a Conservative. That should answer at least two of
your suspicions. And yes, I voted for Nixon. (*Beat.*) Are you a
homosexual?

MIKE

I'm married.

CANDY

So was my father.

MIKE

(*Pause. He takes the cape off her.*) You know, I don't think we can
work together.

CANDY

I am trying to be real.

MIKE

If it's that much of an effort, maybe you should just settle for
artificial.

(*The phone rings.*)

Excuse me.

(*He crosses to the desk and answers curtly.*)

Beauty Parlor, this is Michael. Yes…yes…? Oh, the ad. Yeah, yeah.
I'm sorry, I was distracted. Umm…full time? Well, Saturday's not so
good, we're doing the opening, unless you can make it before
eight…okay. Wait, you know what? I just hired a full-time shampoo
girl, so…okay. Thanks anyway. Bye. (*He returns to his station.*)

CANDY

I've had some time to think, and I've decided to reform.

MIKE

That…*sounds* good.

CANDY

I want to try the curling iron.

MIKE

I can curl your hair without the—

CANDY

No, I want you to use it.

MIKE

You know what? If this is going to work you've got to stop
interrupt—

CANDY

I'm not interrupt—

    (*He glares at her*).

I'm sorry. I…I'm going through something personally difficult right
now, so…it won't happen again.

125

MIKE

How do you plan on avoiding that?

CANDY

I just won't interrupt anymore.

MIKE

Oh, I thought you meant…never mind.

(*Puts his hands on her hair, she stiffens.*)

Just relax. I'm a professional.

(*He picks up a comb, but she grabs his wrist.*)

CANDY

Is that clean?

MIKE

Sterilized according to Board of Health standards.

(*She releases his wrist, and he combs.*)

You've got beautiful hair. Who's been cutting it?

CANDY

Jean Louis.

MIKE

I'm not familiar. In Boston?

CANDY

Newport.

MIKE

Rhode Island?

CANDY

Yes.

MIKE

That's…far.

CANDY

It's an hour's drive. I grew up there. And Newton. Newport-Newton.
You know.

MIKE

Aha. (*He doesn't.*) So you just moved to this area, too. (*Silence.*)
What brings you to—

CANDY

Curiosity.

(*He steps back glaring.*)

I did it again, didn't I? I'm… (*A deep breath—recites her primer.*) I
come from a very solid New England background. The DNA on
Mother's side? D.A.R. Beacon Hill Brahmin and bourbon on Dad's.
We are steeped in tradition here in the birthplace of patriotism. It is
both our mantle and our shroud. Our girls are Miss Porter's School—
we know when to curtsy and we know how to curse—and our boys,
those who are so endowed, are Wall Street and White House bound;
future yachtsmen of the Upper Atlantic. You would do well to attract
members of this select clientele to your new little venture, but
chances are, few will stumble in. The address is wrong.

MIKE

(*Seething.*) So, how does a first-class snob such as yourself happen to stumble in to my humble little "venture" at this undesirable address? Or is that too much to ask someone with such a distinguished pedigree?

CANDY

(*After a beat, simply.*) There is an unmarked storefront around the corner from here where, for three hundred dollars and no questions asked, a girl can rid herself of an unwanted… condition. (*She has gone very pale.*) May I use your restroom, please?

MIKE

(*Getting it.*) Of course. It's right there. You need—?
　　　(*She is up and off left fast.*)

CANDY (off)

Thank you! I'm sorry I interrupt so much.
　　　(*Mike is left alone for a few moments. Bewildered, he pours her a glass of water. Finally, he crosses left to check.*)

MIKE

You okay?

CANDY

(*She re-enters unsteadily.*) Better, thanks.
　　　(*They return to center, Mike supporting her arm. Candy sits.*)

MIKE

(*Handing her the glass of water.*) What's your name, by the way?

CANDY

Candace Dalton. Call me Candy.

MIKE

I'm—

CANDY

You're Mr. Michael, I know. Tsk, damnit, I did it again! Okay, I'm
not all that well-bred. I guess that's how I got into this mess in the
first place.

MIKE

Oh, for crissakes, I don't care. Who's the guy?

(*She glares.*)

Is he involved is what I meant to ask. You don't have to—

(*She opens her mouth and he stops her.*)

Shush!

(*She smiles.*)

Don't tell me anything you don't want to. I just hope you told *him.*

CANDY

Well, I didn't. His name is Maurice. He just started Harvard Business
School. It's a bad time for him to have to deal with something like
this.

MIKE

As opposed to the girl he knocked up. Must be a great time for you to
have to go it alone, huh?

(*She doesn't answer.*)

Was it painful?

CANDY

I haven't done it yet. I was scheduled to this morning, but I…well, something drew me here instead, so I ducked in.

MIKE

I'm happy you did. What kind of work do you do?

CANDY

I'm hoping to get into TV.

MIKE

You're pretty enough. Wow, acting. My cousin's an act—

CANDY

Oh, God no. I'd like to do something important. Broadcast journalism. Producing. Going through private school, you tend to forget that there's a world out there full of things you've been insulated from.

MIKE

Like?

CANDY

I don't know. Civil rights. The Vietnam War. I have no idea where Vietnam is, do you?

(*He's silent.*)

And I've had a formal education. It's pathetic. I know how to set a table, make a man feel like he's the center of the world—

MIKE

Uh, my turn to interrupt. (*Thinks better.*) Let's just talk about hair. (*He goes for his book of samples—drawings he's done of trendy hairdos.*)

CANDY

You're different.

MIKE

Because I went to beauty school, not Princeton?

CANDY

Just because. I can tell. Maybe it's your upbringing. You're a nice man. What church do you go to?

(*Dissembling, he turns pages of his book to show her.*)

MIKE

So…? Are we going to send that pageboy back to 1955 or shall I heat up some bronze so you can mount it next to your baby shoes?

CANDY

That's not nice.

MIKE

No, that's business. Jean Louis may have been good for your Mama, but baby… (*He steps back, appraising. Beat.*) You know what I think?

CANDY

I'm afraid to guess.

MIKE

I think you'd look fantastic no matter what I did.

CANDY

(*Blushing.*) You're going to do very well here in Framingham.

MIKE

Don't invite the kenahora.

(*She's puzzled.*)

You don't know many Jews, do you? Alright, can I just fantasize a moment?

CANDY

With your eyes open, please.

MIKE

You've got great symmetry with these features… (*An artist at work, he strokes the air around her face.*) …and this line is classic… (*More air strokes.*) …an asymmetrical cut with just some subtle frosting… (*In air.*) …here and here, and mark my words, you'll stop traffic.

CANDY

Is that something I should aspire to?

(*He stands back with an "Are you kidding?" gesture. It makes her laugh.*)

Alright, Michelangelo. But if you make me look deranged, I'll bring you up on charges.

MIKE

(*Laughs.*) I'd go to court just to hear what those might be.

CANDY

They'd include scalping, hatcheting, or any effects achieved with a blunt instrument.

MIKE

Lady! Haven't you heard? This is the dawning of the Age of Aquarius?

(*Sally walks through loaded down with paper bags, spilling.*)

SALLY

You said Chock Full o' Nuts, right? They were out of olive loaf. That fuckin' market is full of hairy eyeballs starin' at my ass...

(*Mike and Candy burst out laughing. Music swells, "Age of Aquarius" by The 5th Dimension: "This is the dawning of the Age of Aquarius..."*

Lights change. Candy and Sally exit. Mike, at the reception desk, talks on the phone to his wife, Becky.)

MIKE

(*On phone.*) ...her name is Candy...the opposite, *high* class...yeah, my first customer and her name is Candy, can you believe that? No, she won't spoil my appetite. She's in bad shape, emotionally, but...you know there's an abortion clinic around the corner from here? Yeah, it freaks me out, too...no, she was about to...well, even educated kids from tony families make stupid mistakes, right? Once she gets it together and finds her heart, I bet she'll be unstoppable.

She's a knockout…no, I don't have a crush on her, Becky, I have a *customer*. Becky! Will you stop it? …uh-huh…uh-huh…okay, wifey. Uh-huh…when? Uh-huh…really? Hmm…

> (*Candy emerges with same hair but a different frock as Mike continues grunting in response to his wife's conversation.*)

CANDY

(*To audience.*) So…that was the beginning. 1969. Crazy transition time for me. For anyone alive, I'd say. Forgive me, but for those of you who weren't born yet you will just have to trust me. Google it. 1969. That summer: Woodstock, first man on the moon, the Manson Murders, all in about three weeks' time. And then there was that little news item about Stonewall. Little did we know we were all about to make a grand jeté into a decade of social experimentation. Little did we realize the seventies would land us dead center on the disco floor. More on that in a minute.

MIKE

(*Finishes up his phone conversation.*) Mm-hmm…did you get my Salems? Alright…is that the baby crying? Well, give him the bottle. Okay, I'll pick up a case of Enfamil on my way home. Bye.

> (*He dances off, she watching and then turning back to audience.*)

CANDY

I walked out of Salon Élan a little less heavy-hearted that day. And I looked it. Well, my hair did. For a few days, I actually considered being a single mom. Wasn't meant to be, though. The stigma at that time was untenable. So, after procrastinating…my best friend, Joanne, drove me back to Framingham and… (*Takes a deep breath, gestures to audience.*) …this is one way I can process it. I have Mike to thank for that. I swear, that wasn't a comb in his hand, it was a magic wand. So I started booking appointments. I became a "regular" as they say, and in the process I learned a lot about the "Merlin" behind the chair.

(*She sits in his chair as Mike re-enters with a styling cape. Stevie Wonder's "Superstition" plays.*)

FYI, it's now 1972…

Scene 2

CANDY

(*To Mike.*) They're offering me travel editor for the PBS affiliate in Boston.

MIKE

(*As he primps.*) I told you! Mazel tov. You'll be on NBC in no time, and you better give me credit…on national TV.

CANDY

(*Pause, as she thinks it over.*) What makes you think a network would want me?

MIKE

You're drop dead gorgeous. Stop-traffic gorgeous. And you're smart.

CANDY

Like the seven thousand applicants they hear from daily.

MIKE

Hey, what do they know? *I* know. I've been to art school, so aesthetics hold a central place in my life. You are aesthetically pleasing.

CANDY

(*Blushing.*) Thanks to a certain man of hair.

> (*Sally rushes in from stage right entrance, breathless and disheveled.*)

136

SALLY

Sorry I'm late, Mike. Larry got caught car-jacking at the Loggins and Messina concert and his sister wouldn't put up the bail. (*Exits to sinks left.*)

CANDY

(*Of Sally.*) How's that working out?

MIKE

Hard work? A+. Private life? D-. I keep pushing her toward night classes. (*He primps around her head, then notices a big rock on her finger.*) Wait, what's that?!

CANDY

Oh, that? 'Bout time you noticed. That's…Phil.

MIKE

(*Lifting her hand.*) Hello-o, Phil. Obviously, Phil does not work for the postal service.

CANDY

(*Shakes head no.*) Shipping.

MIKE

As in, "and Receiving"?
   (*She shakes head again.*)
Oh, as in Onassis.

CANDY

Closer. (*Pulls hand away.*) Mind your business. He's Maurice's cousin.

MIKE

On the moneyed side, apparently. So it's all in the family. Smart girl.

(*He goes back to her hair.*) Do I get to meet "Money Bags"?

CANDY

Not today you don't. We're in football playoffs. Dallas Cowboys…

MIKE

Ah, yes. Good old Guy Lombardi.

CANDY

VINCE Lombardi. Get your coaches straight. Vince is Green Bay, and dead.

MIKE

Hmm…maybe *I* should be in night school.

CANDY

(*Beat.*) Why did you leave art school, Mike? Those hairdo sketches you do are awfully good. You've got real talent.

MIKE

(*Wince—painful memory.*) Yes, I was considered a good artist…by my family. I was okay, I guess, but…circumstances propelled me into the beauty business.

CANDY

Circumstances?

(*He turns away.*)

Alright, I'm not one to pry. But after everything you've gotten out of me since day one…I think you owe me.

MIKE

I had a little…problem. Okay? What you might call a pathology. It's always been there, but it…I guess it bloomed in art school. (*This is not easy.*)

CANDY

You know we don't have to talk about—

(*He opens his station drawer and takes out a black and white photograph—two men. Hands it to her.*)

Is that you? Oh, my God, a pompadour? And matching suits… pegged pants!

(*She reads the date on the side.*)

1957. Sure was. Who's the blond?

MIKE

Johnny Kearny. (*Lights a cigarette.*)

CANDY

Irish. A toughie. You two were ladykillers.

MIKE

(*Snatching the photo back.*) No ladies were harmed in the making of this picture. (*He puts it back in his drawer, turns to look at her.*)

CANDY

Oh, Mike…you were in love with him. Was he in art school with you?

MIKE

I was sick, Candy.

CANDY

Mike, I don't think…why would you keep that photo in your drawer if—

CENTER

MIKE

It's a mental illness. Check the American Psychiatric Association's diagnostic criteria. We did.

CANDY

You and—?

MIKE

My parents.

CANDY

So, what? You saw a psychiatrist?

MIKE

Dr. Leshkoff—he liked to be called "Irv"—prescribed the only corrective therapy he deemed foolproof. And my well-intentioned but uneducated parents followed his plan. (*He can't talk about this.*) Have you ever considered going red?

CANDY

(*With great sympathy.*) Mike, you didn't…you don't ever have to tell me what you went through. Really.

MIKE

(*From the hip.*) Electroshock therapy. Bellevue. Three times a week. We took the Flatbush Avenue bus, Mom and I. There and back. That's what I'm told. I don't remember the coming back part.

(*Mike goes back to working on Candy's hair. Silence. A long pause. Finally, she arrests his hand.*)

CANDY

I'm sorry they listened to Irv.

MIKE

He had some nerve.

CANDY

Calling you a perv.

> (*They share a good laugh, breaking the solemnity. His work*
> *resumes.*)

I'm happy you told me. I'm glad to know.

MIKE

Why? Make you feel better about something?

CANDY

Us. (*Ruminating.*) And…my father. (*Off his look.*) I've mentioned this. Darling Spencer Dalton, from the bluest blood on Beacon Hill, who spends most of the year on Mykonos now, paddling around the Aegean while nimble young Greek boys dive for his…his wallet. The wreck of the SS Daddy. He chose immersion therapy for his pathology's cure.

MIKE

He could afford to. (*Back to work.*) Anyway, making art and doing hair are not that different really, except that…in art, the moment you complete something your work doesn't turn around and ask for "a little more off the bangs, please." And there are no tips. Can't beat the instant gratification of cash in hand every day. Hair is seductive

141

that way. (*Beat.*) Are you listening, Miss "Less-Than-Ten-Percent"?

CANDY

Are you calling me a tightwad?

MIKE

I'm just sayin'…with your refined tastes, I'd keep my eye on a network job if I were you. Phil or no Phil.

(*She stabs at his waist with her finger.*)

Ow!

(*She stabs at him again and keeps stabbing.*)

What? I know the score. You're fiscally conservative, that's all. You're a Nixon Girl. You're against socialized medicine and food stamps, which is exactly what *I'm* going to have to stock up on to keep my kids fed on your lousy tips—stop!

CANDY

(*Getting out of the chair, a playful pursuit.*) You're a rat-fink and I hate you!

MIKE

Ooo, really? Oh, damn, I forgot to sterilize this comb!

CANDY

I hate you!

MIKE

Cooties on you!

(*Lights change as she chases him around the chair and off.*)

Scene 3

(1975, the Average White Band's "Pick Up the Pieces" plays. Chattering voices. Busy place. Sally, now visibly pregnant, sweeps insouciantly, occasionally swiveling her hips in time with music. She speaks her thoughts out loud to an offstage Mike.)

SALLY

…and I don't know, Mike. I guess it's kinda like when you like someone, but they're, like, space cadets, but you, like, like them anyway. And you do all this stupid stuff. You know, to like, *show* them. And then you're like, what the…? 'Cause, like, it's so obvious to all your friends, even the spazzy twerpazoids who flunked Home Ec., that like, this ape in espadrilles has, like, zero interest in anything that doesn't resemble him.

(A phone starts ringing. She's oblivious.)

And it's like, God, I could be like doing squat thrusts on the hood of his Pinto from here to Filene's Basement and he wouldn't even turn his wipers on. And I'm like…*Larry!*

(The phone continues ringing. Enter Mike, now 37, with tinted glasses, a faux 'fro, a mustache, bell-bottoms, white boots—very Sonny of "& Cher" fame. A cigarette dangles.)

MIKE

(*To Sally, in passing.*) Stop saying "like."

    (*As he answers phone, Sally exits, sweeping, off left.*)

(*On phone.*) Salon Élan…this is Mr. Michael….sure, Natalie, one sec… (*Checking book.*) I've got 10:30 open on Thursday morning …no, the night is gone…I'll put you in for 10:30 and if there's a cancellation I'll move you…wait a sec… (*Calling off.*) Sally, get Francie out of the dryer and rinse Mrs. Hammerslag before that perm solution eats through her scalp. (*Back to phone.*) Sorry, what? Yeah, we've got plenty of pink rinse on hand…no, it's Roux…I know, but I didn't do the ordering last month, I was in jail, remember?

    (*Candy, now 30, enters. Different. Stylish. A knockout. She's
    just back from a shopping spree in Paris but "dressed down"
    in platforms, kerchief, sunglasses and Jordache. Michael
    waves and motions her to the sinks but she stays put.*)

(*Still on phone.*) No, no more drinking and driving. Daddy learned his lesson. Yeah, only when I'm on skates. I gotta go, I got a bridal party here. (*Winks at Candy.*) Okay, Thursday. Bye.

    (*He hangs up the phone, which rings intermittently
    throughout, and moves behind Candy, putting both hands on
    her hips to steer her to the sinks. She resists.*)

(*Singing.*) "Here comes the bride, all dressed in…"

CANDY

(*Hands him a small box.*) I have to talk to you.

MIKE

In the chair. I'm behind, and you're due at St. Blaise's in two hours.

CANDY

(*Holding her ground.*) What happened with Joanne?

MIKE

Why, what did she tell you?

CANDY

She's not talking to me.

MIKE

(*Dissembling.*) She had root canal.

CANDY

That wouldn't stop her, she's my best friend.

MIKE

Candy, she's a total pain in the— Last night she was the only member of your bridal party who— Look, I'm backing up. Get changed and I'll explain.

CANDY

(*Moving closer.*) You've got a lot of explaining to do, Mister. (*In his face.*) Start talking!

MIKE

(*At his chair, unflinching.*) I kicked her out.

CANDY

You WHAT?!

MIKE

I don't need the tsuris. (*Beat.*) She's after your groom, Candy.

CANDY

(*Uncomprehending.*) How do you know that?

MIKE

You should have heard her this morning. I told her to lay off Phil since he's yours as of this afternoon and you know what she had the nerve to say to me? "With a busybody like you around they could change this town's name to Faggyham."

CANDY

When did this happen?

MIKE

Ten minutes ago. I hurled her out, curlers flying everywhere—

CANDY

She's my maid of honor!

MIKE

Get another one! She's got split ends anyway. Fuck her.

(*Candy starts to cry.*)

You're crying over Joanne?

(*She shakes head.*)

What? Not Maurice again?

(*She nods.*)

You people…

CANDY

(*Sucking it up.*) Maurice got Phil so drunk at the bachelor party last night he's still throwing up. Then he came over to my place.

MIKE

Phil did?

(*She shakes her head no.*)

Maurice came o—?

(*Nods yes.*)

Candy, you're an addict. Six years that guy has been fucking you over…I don't want hear this… (*He covers his ears.*) La-la-la-la-la—

CANDY

(*Overlapping.*) I can't get married today. She can have Phil. I'm still too obsessed with his damn cousin…oh Mike, it's grand opera. Save me! Throw me off a turret!

MIKE

Hey, Tosca.

(*She bucks up.*)

I'm a simple barber from the Island they call Long. Do me a favor? Breathe. Hold your nose…

(*She does.*)

…long breath, through the mouth…

(*She does.*)

Good girl. Now read my lips: Marry Phil today, as planned.

(*She dissolves again.*)

C'mon, *Phil's* the guy who can provide for those kids you say you want. He's rolling in it.

(*She shakes her head no, but he takes her by the chin.*)

When Maurice got you pregnant all those years ago what did you do? You terminated it because it wasn't a good time…for *him*. It'll never be a good time for him, Candy. He's a climber. Besides, I met him. One glance is all it took. Maurice will sleep with anything that has lips. I should know. (*Purses lips.*) Go get changed.

CANDY

What do you mean, "You should know"? You didn't sleep with…?

(*He shrugs.*)

Not while he was with me.

MIKE

(*A devil's grin.*) You want the details, *go change.*

CANDY

(*Like the D.A.*) Where's the birthmark?

MIKE

Candy—

CANDY

Maurice has a prominent birthmark in a surprising place, where is it?

(*He smiles.*)

Someday I'm gonna put that rattail comb right through your heart.

MIKE

What heart?

CANDY

(*Stalking off to change.*) I'll have you castrated!

MIKE

Not if you want this installed properly. (*He pulls paper off the box.*) My God, it's Fabergé…

(*He carefully lifts the tiara out, gasps, sings.*)

"Here comes the bride…"

(*As phone starts ringing, Sally enters from sink area.*)

SALLY

(*Sotto voce.*) Mike, that bitch didn't tip me last night.

(*He points at phone. Begrudgingly, Sally answers it.*)

Salon Élan, this is Star… (*Hand over receiver.*) Psst…your wife is on the phone.

(*He tries not to, then…*)

MIKE

(*On phone, distracted.*) Becky? Busy, what? …well, put some ointment on it…how bad? …didja call the doctor? …to the emergency room? I can't! I've got a bridal party…well, you shouldn't have left a hot iron where he could reach it…

(*Sally eavesdrops.*)

Oh, for crissakes, Becky, when are you going to forgive me for that…no, don't go to your sister's…I'll call you back in a half hour. Put some Bactine on his hand. I promise, I'll call…okay, bye. (*He hangs up.*) Goddamnit!

SALLY

(*Following.*) Everything alrigh—?

MIKE

(*Throws her car keys.*) Get me my Quaaludes. They're in the glove compartment.

(*She hesitates.*)

Just hurry up.

(*She starts off.*)

They're in the aspirin jar. And the Tums, too. My stomach is burning. Don't steal any!

(*Sally exits. Mike turns up the radio, adjusts himself in mirror, restoring his people-pleasing self as Candy, now composed, re-enters in styling cape. He seats her in his chair. She can't help reacting to the sound of a radio news report...*)

NEWS REPORTER (V.O.)

"Sentencing begins today for John Mitchell, John Erlichman, and H.R. Haldeman, bringing the final chapter of Richard Nixon's Watergate scandal to a close, while in Great Britain, leader of the Conservative Party Margaret Thatcher succeeds Edward Heath as Prime Minister. In New York, Teamsters leader Jimmy Hoffa is still missing, while in San Francisco,   publishing heiress Patricia Hearst has been found...details at eleven. This is W-GAY... (*Segue/disco.*) ...keepin' the chili in Beantown."

(*Sally re-enters with the drugs.*)

MIKE

Lower that radio, Sal.

SALLY

(*As she does.*) Where do you want your candy?

(*Candy turns.*)

Not you, the real stuff.

(*Mike scowls, takes the pill jar from Sally. She exits. Mike takes pill. He begins applying finishing touches to Candy's classic coif, the tiara still on his station. Candy hands bobby pins. There is a palpable chill between them, which he tries to bypass.*)

MIKE

So? Paris? How was it?

CANDY

French.

MIKE

(*He steps back.*) Look, the shit with Joanne, I'm…I'm sor—

CANDY

(*She stops him.*) Nevermind! Drop it. I have. Ask me about France.

MIKE

Fashion week?

CANDY

(*Coming out of torpor.*) Oh, God it was so gorgeous. The affiliates had me on the top floor of this tiny little hotel called the Récamier, near Saint-Sulpice on the Left Bank. It's where Parisians supposedly go when they're having affairs. Thank God the stupid kids didn't firebomb it in the riots of '68. Such beauty that it changes you from within. By the last day, I managed to negotiate an interview with Ian Wright from Neiman Marcus. We drank Veuve Clicquot at Brasserie Lipp. He took me shopping—that tiara was his find. The shops are incredible, Mike. You'd die. We wound up walking along the Seine, the sun setting at like ten thirty. And then, fireworks, like you've never seen! You really have to get over there, Michael. I mean, c'mon. The Louvre, Mona Lisa—

MIKE

She's got lousy hair.

CANDY

Nitwit. You call yourself an *artiste*? You haven't traveled more than fifteen minutes from behind this chair in the six years since I've been coming here.

MIKE

I go into Boston.

CANDY

To cruise the Fenway.

MIKE

Hey, now…

CANDY

You told me you were there on Sunday.

MIKE

(*Indignant.*) To *shop*…

CANDY

(*Under breath.*) For queers—

MIKE

For *shears,* I said…on Newbury Street. And we don't say "queers" anymore.

CANDY

I know. "Gay." Woop-dee-do! Let's call National Geographic! Better yet, let's call your wife.

MIKE

Becky and I are…we're negotiating our differences.

CANDY

(*She smirks.*) You are the only man I know who can sound like Henry Kissinger and dress like Liza Minnelli.

MIKE

Thank you. The customer's approval makes all the labor worthwhile.

CANDY

(*Appraising his handiwork in the mirror.*) I like this.

MIKE

Next wedding, maybe you'll invite the help.

CANDY

I… (*Beat as she reconsiders, then.*) Did you really do Maurice?

MIKE

Of course not! I saw him *once* when he came to pick you up.
Besides, he's not my type. Too lanky.

(*She smacks him.*)

Incidentally, did you ever tell him about…?

(*She looks at him.*)

You didn't. Some wolves get to ride for free. (*He carefully sets the
tiara in place on her head.*) Nice. (*Showing her herself.*) Look,
M'Lady.

(*She's nonplussed.*)

Okay, I'll live vicariously then.

CANDY

You're lucky you're living at all after firing my maid of honor.

MIKE

Dis-honor.

CANDY

(*Appraising herself.*) Mike, why would a dear old friend like Joanne
try to sabotage me today?

MIKE

You kidding? You're marrying old money from Chestnut Hill. Your
own mother would hire hit men to get a piece of that. Forget the
limo, I'd ride in a tank.

CANDY

Doesn't anybody feel glad anymore when good things happen to friends?

MIKE

It's 1975, Pollyanna, not the Summer of Love. Wake up, the experiment failed. Besides, we're talking Joanne. No amount of therapy will ever make up for the love she didn't get as a kid.

(*Finished, he sits beside her.*)

She's a vacuum, and I'm not talking Electrolux.

(*He snorts imaginary coke; she stares blankly.*)

You have no idea what I'm talking—

CANDY

(*Pretending no clue.*) A Hoover? (*Pressing on.*) When I think of how much time I spent helping her out. When her father died—

MIKE

So learn. Good Samaritans only make people mad, Candy. They accentuate our guilt.

(*She starts tearing up again.*)

Stop that. Get out of my chair.

(*He removes her cape. She won't budge. He opens his drawer.*)

Okay, you want a little something to get you through today?

CANDY

Like what? (*Blows her nose.*) A handgun?

MIKE

Better. (*He shows her the "Aspirin" jar, shakes it.*) Mother's little helper.

CANDY

What's that?

(*He simply nods and swivels his hips.*)

I could have you arrested.

MIKE

Promise?

(*She grabs the jar, pours it into her hand.*)

Just one! It'll smooth all the edges.

(*He crosses for water.*)

Chaser?

CANDY

(*Beat.*) Okay. Fuck Joanne, and fuck Maurice.

(*She downs the pill. He offers her water. She drinks.*)

MIKE

Voilà!

CANDY

(*Beat, then, of the Quaalude.*) How long does it take?

(*Mike smiles. She stands and primps in mirror.*)

Joanne, Joanne, Joanne. She's always competed with me. If I buy blue eye-shadow, she runs out to buy *indigo*. If I—

MIKE

Enough with Joanne! All God's make-up and all God's hair cannot disguise the ultraviolet glow of her self-loathing. (*He takes her by the wrist.*) If you don't stop fidgeting with my masterpiece I'm going to set your hair on fire. (*With a free hand he flicks his Bic lighter.*)

CANDY

I love it when you go all macho.

MIKE

Ah, the 'lude intrudes. (*Lighting a cigarette.*) Go, get outta here. I gotta call my wife.

(*She reaches for her purse as she drifts unsteadily toward the reception area, then stops to giggle.*)

CANDY

I think I feel tingly. Oh, shit, Mike. I only have francs. Can I pay you next time?

MIKE

(*With heavy Italian dialect.*) ROBBERY! AYUDA! AYUDA! SOMEBODY STOP HER!

(*Sally enters, broom raised at the ready to defend him.*)

HELP, SALLY! THIS-A BRIDE, SHE'S-A ROBBING ME! THIS-A BRIDE ROBS EVERYBODY!

(*Sally gets the joke and exits, not amused. Mike turns back to Candy, sans accent, kissing her hand.*)

Go, and be wed.

(As lights come down, a spotlight comes up, downstage right, on Candy, who giggles as she speaks to the audience.)

CANDY

Mike's Quaalude got me through an otherwise intolerable day, or who knows what I might have…? Who knew taking vows could be such a scream? Strangely, no one else found them funny. Oh, Phil got into the swing of it—he was still blottoed from the night before—but his mother, the Countess Sarcophagus, was fit to be tied. I can't really blame her. I look cross-eyed in all the wedding shots. Just a harbinger of the farce to come. Oh, and one final footnote on Joanne: Neither she nor Maurice were seen again. Word came back they took off for the Naropa Institute in Boulder, Colorado the very day of my nuptials. Yes, the dish ran away with the spoon. And Mike? Well, I couldn't have invited him to my wedding. He would have stood out like a hot pink boa on Betty Friedan. Funny, I don't know how he did it but over the years Mike was able to seduce me into giving him eyewitness accounts of each episode of my misspent youth, while he remained safely ensconced at his station. Wild horses could not pry him out from behind that chair. Oh, we tried hanging out in the real world… once—

MIKE (off)

(Yelling.) TWICE!

CANDY

Twice? *(To Mike.)* When, twice? We had you and Becky over for cocktails and cards… (*Back out.*) That was a disaster. Phil was in one of his moods… (*Indicates tipping back a glass.*) …Becky got smashed and wet herself laughing. Poor Becky. It was so obvious Mike found his marriage…shall we say *limiting*? If I recall correctly, he was wearing more bling that night than Becky and I combined.

MIKE (off)

WE WENT TO THE DISCO!

CANDY

Oh, that's right—he took me dancing one night at Chaps when Phil was in rehab. Another disaster. The bottom rung of self-esteem. What *does* a straight woman wear to an all-male disco? Those boys were prettier than me!

MIKE (off)

THEY ALL LOVED YOU!

CANDY

(*Replies.*) I WAS PREMENSTRUAL! (*Back out.*) I had post-nasal drip. Everyone's nose was dripping. Mine from a cold. Mike was so kind that night…come to think of it, it wasn't out of kindness that he lent me his car that night. (*She leans in confidentially.*) He's got a thing for chubby redheads, and there was—

> (*Mike re-enters, now in a short platinum David Bowie wig
> with an asymmetrical cut, one side hanging over an eye.
> Continuing the Ziggy Stardust theme, he wears a purple,
> short-waisted bolero jacket with shoulder pads over a red T-*

159

shirt, high-waisted pegged pants, a silver cummerbund and

matching silver combat boots.)

MIKE

You are way out of line, sister.

CANDY

You do.

MIKE

Buster was not chubby. He was wearing cargo pants.

CANDY

(*To audience.*) Right.

MIKE

You exaggerate. This is why we can't hang out.

(*She gives the audience a "Jack Benny" and exits up left*

toward sinks. When she's gone, Mike turns on the radio—

Prince's "Controversy"—and begins tidying up.)

Scene 4

(*As the scene progresses, Mike makes his way to his station and cleans combs and brushes. He calls off.*)

MIKE

Seriously…if you're going to insist on our *not* falling out…

(*Candy pokes her head out—or in V.O.—and addresses audience.*)

CANDY

It's around 1983, I think. Yeah, cause Reagan has just started campaigning for a second term.

(*She disappears again. Continuous sound of water, off.*)

MIKE

(*As he preps at station.*) Why are you voting for him again?

CANDY (off)

He makes economic sense!

MIKE

Look, I don't care that you're a Republican…

CANDY (off)

LIAR!

MIKE

Even Gorbachev has a bigger heart than that bozo.

CANDY (off)

So move to Moscow!

MIKE

(*Picking up a tearsheet from a magazine of the day that Candy gave him.*) And you know what? That Norma Kamali look is not for you.

CANDY (off)

What's that got to do with Ronald Reagan?

MIKE

I don't know. Everything! The shoulder pads, the pompadour, the braid down the back, the leg warmers and heels…you'd look insane.

CANDY (off)

Look who's talking, Ziggy Stardust. Is there life on Mars?

MIKE

Bowie is a trendsetter! You know who you look like? My ex-wife.

CANDY (off)

Ex-? Since when is Becky "ex-"? (*To Sally, who's washing her hair.*) OW! Could you lower the temperature a little below scalding please?

SALLY (off)

Hey, talk to your stylist! He's the one with the lacquer can. I gotta melt it.

MIKE

(*Having overheard.*) SAL! (*Beat.*) Becky and I separated last month. We've been negotiating through pretty bad feelings for a long time and the decibel level of anger and resentment has been unbearable. Did I tell you she's dating an ex-Black Panther? And of course the kids are acting out now—in school, at the table— So…I got a condo

162

off Route 9. I'm dedicating myself to full-time promiscuity. It'll be amazing if I have any skin left... (*Sotto voce.*) ...*down there.* How are you and Phil doing? (*No answer.*) Thought so. Truth be told, the seams seem to be splitting for every couple I know. All over America, *your* President's promise of an economic boom is tearing families limb from limb. (*Beat.*) You listening? I've been watching Tom Brokaw and Jane Pauley every morning. You? (*No answer. To self.*) Well, boom or bust, families are always first to show the strain. (*Still just the sound of running water off.*) Sally, what are you doing, hosing her whole body down?

> (*Candy enters, fit to be tied, in towel turban, doffing styling cape. She is very Norma Kamali. She grabs her purse.*)

CANDY

Enough with the abuse, I'm out of here.

MIKE

What now? Where you going? (*Calling off.*) SAL!

CANDY

And where the hell were you last Friday night?

MIKE

Who can remember that far back? Probably on my knees behind some bush.

CANDY

(*Dead serious.*) Not funny, Mike. When I call you on your home phone and leave you *three* messages, it's urgent. I expect you to get back to me.

MIKE

Whoa, whoa, *whoa*—! Take a Valium, darling.

CANDY

Do you remember that I had an invitation to the Governor's Ball? Do you remember that I had helped launch Ed King's campaign to curb property taxes in this district? Do you appreciate the fact that you're saving a substantial amount on your *two* properties thanks to my initiative on your behalf?

MIKE

(*Taken aback.*) Sorry, I'm not in a courtier's frame of mind, my dear.

CANDY

Next time, call me. I looked like a hausfrau that night.

(*She storms out. Mike walks off toward sinks.*)

MIKE

Sally? I don't what you did but slip a laxative into her coffee next Saturday before you do it again, will ya? I'm getting cigs. (*Exits.*)

(**ENTR'ACTE**—*A segue of time…Eurythmics' "Sweet Dreams (Are Made of This)." Sally, dressed very Pat Benatar—headband and spandex, rollerskates—adjusts the set, sweeps vigorously…speedy. Finally landing at the desk, she calls off.*)

SALLY

So, Mike…Frannie Mandelbaum keeps calling about this 9:30 slot. You want me to fill it, or you… (*Under breath.*) …holding out some

164

weird, perverted hope? (*She opens the appointment book, writes in Frannie's name.*)

MIKE (off)

It's been three months, Sal. I can't believe Candy would just disappear.

SALLY

Yeah, well…the only problem is you're booked solid, so if you do take Frannie and Miss Thing strolls in… (*Beat.*) So, what do you wanna do?

MIKE (off)

Write Frannie in. But you know what, Sal? No matter how busy I get, come Saturday morning I'll never stop looking toward that door. I just know it.

SALLY

(*Rolling eyes.*) Maybe she's sampling the competition…I hear André, the Romanian at Didi's SnipTease is hot.

(*He hisses. Under her breath.*)

Or maybe she got hit by a bus.

(*Then, stealthily, Candy sneaks back onstage, repentant and sheepish, sporting a terrible hairdo circa the Reagan Era. She scurries past Sally, head bowed, hands clasped in prayer, and slips back to the supply room where Mike is. He shrieks…*)

165

MIKE (off)

HIDEOUS! THE HORROR, THE HORROR!

SALLY

(*Scanning appointment book, under breath.*) And lucky for her, you
have an opening. (*Erasing a name.*) Bye-bye, Frannie Mandelbaum.

CANDY (off)

I'm so, so sorry.

MIKE (off)

You know the drill…to the sinks! Sally!

SALLY

SHIT! (*Sally skates off toward the sinks.*)

Scene 5

(*1984. 9:30 a.m., another Saturday in February. Same salon, different decor. The layout of the shop hasn't changed, just its style. The music segues into a news reporter's broadcast as Sally returns to adjust the set.*)

NEWS REPORTER (V.O.)

"It is now estimated that as many as twenty-five hundred people may have died in Bhopal, India as a result of the toxic gas leak from the Union Carbide Plant there. In other news, President Reagan returns today from his visit to Normandy commemorating the fortieth anniversary of the Allied invasion. And soul singer Marvin Gaye has been shot dead in his Los Angeles home by his father. He was forty-six. This is WQXR-FM 93 in Boston. The time is 9:33, February 4th, 1984..."

(*Sound: Marvin Gaye's "Sexual Healing." Sally calls her son.*)

SALLY

(*On phone.*) Finney? It's Mommy...I know, honey. I'm sorry... no, I'm still at work...I know. As soon as she gets here I'll jump in the car...Finney?

(*Her son hung up. As she redials, enter Mike, a.k.a. Mikey Z: dangling cigarette, Don Johnson suit, shoulder pads, sleeves pushed up, skinny tie or T-shirt, his hair is bouffant. Has he been snorting something? Sally is on him.*)

SALLY

Mike, Heather didn't show up yet, but I can't fill in for her this morning. Finney's getting his green belt and I promised him I would be there…

(*He turns away.*)

Mike…? I *told* you…

MIKE

I'm running a business, Sal. You're a hairdresser now. You got appointments. Who's going to—?

SALLY

(*Loud.*) Mike!

(*He stops, turns.*)

Okay, I *really* gotta talk to you.

MIKE

You're not amping up on that devil dust anymore, are you Sal? You got a kid now. Let me see your gums.

SALLY

I told you I quit when I got pregnant the first time.

MIKE

The *first* time?

SALLY

Yeah, so…that's what I'm tryin' to tell ya. You can put two and two together, can't ya?

MIKE

(*Realizing.*) Sally...again? How long?

SALLY

It's just the first trimester.

MIKE

Different guy.

(*The phone starts ringing.*)

SALLY

Yeah, but he's another jerk, so he's already history.

MIKE

You're supposed to learn from history, Sal. Masterpiece Theatre, Episode Two.

SALLY

I won't miss much work if that's what's botherin' ya. My mother's movin' in to help out. Now can you just let me—

MIKE

(*Turning away.*) Shampoo Candy when she gets in, then you can go.

(*She sweeps, disgruntled, as Mike answers the phone.*)

(*On phone.*) StarCutz, this is Mikey Z...oh, hi Sondra...good, 'n' you? (*Laughing.*) Yeah, well it's April in Massachusetts. It took me forty-five minutes, with chains! Okay...no, you're the third cancellation ...if it's clear by tonight...no, nothing else for two weeks at least...you leave when? Damn you snowbirds...alright, I'll squeeze you in Tuesday. Give me your number. (*He writes.*) No, I'll call, I promise. Hey, invite me down some time—Boca sounds like heaven… (*Hand over receiver.*) I'd rather swallow lye.

> (*Candy enters, fully outfitted for winter in full-length coat, a mink hat, sunglasses. She looks distraught. She slides off her kid gloves, undoes coat. Michael waves, finishes call.*)

God, no! I don't fly! I'm terrified…maybe by car. Yeah…my next is here…yeah…I'll call! Yeah…Sondra, I said I'll call, I'LL CALL! Bye. (*Hangs up.*) Oof, that one can bend your ear. (*Noticing she's inert.*) What's the matter?

CANDY

Did you hear about Marvin Gaye?

MIKE

I know. Horrible, right? Get washed.

CANDY

I washed it myself.

> (*Sally, thrilled, exits.*)

His own father.

MIKE

It's usually the kid with the gun. Why'd you wash it? (*Beat.*) Give me your coat…

> (*She does, slipping out of coat to reveal sweats. As he helps her with her coat, she takes off her sunglasses and turns to reveal a bruised jaw. Mike gasps.*)

What the hell happened to you?

CANDY

(*Putting glasses back on.*) It was an accident.

MIKE

Car?

CANDY

(*Hesitant.*) Gin.

MIKE

(*Beat.*) Phil.

CANDY

(*Sigh.*) I don't want to be married anymore.

MIKE

(*Leading her to his chair and calling off left.*) Sally, get me some ice cubes and wrap them in a towel. (*Seating Candy. With German accent.*) Come, talk. Dr. Wuth iz nozing but ears for da bwuised shiksa.

> (*She settles in his chair, not laughing. Beat. Dropping accent.*)

Is this the first time?

CANDY

He's pushed me around before, but...

MIKE

So, it's not.

CANDY

I swear to God, it's his father. Phil never should have gone to work for that son-of-a-bitch. The Greek shipping guys are all tyrants. I told him that. Now he blames me.

MIKE

For telling the truth? (*Beat.*) How much time you giving yourself
these days?

CANDY

What do you mean?

MIKE

Aside from this… (*Holds up comb.*) …what are you doing that's
feeding *you*? (*Silence.*) You're not coming up with a good reason to
stick around, are you?

CANDY

I took a vow, Mike. Just because you walked out of your marriage
you think everyone should.

MIKE

I never should have gotten married. Not with my true nature… such
as it is.

CANDY

Told that to your kids lately?

MIKE

They're still too young to know.

CANDY

Danny's fourteen, isn't he? You knew your "true nature" by fourteen.

MIKE

In the fifties? We didn't have true natures then. They only just started distributing those.

CANDY

(*A rueful smile.*) So, maybe I need to walk away from this.

MIKE

It only takes two feet, Candy. Hold on a sec…

    (*Sally enters in her coat with a cold compress. He removes Candy's glasses and places the compress on her black eye. She winces. Mike glares at Sally exiting off right, looking over her shoulder.*)

You could move in with me.

    (*Candy laughs.*)

No, really. I've got a guest room in the condo.

CANDY

I thought that's where your kids stay.

MIKE

Weekends. They can use the sofa bed.

CANDY

That's a very sweet offer, but no, thank you. I don't think my true nature could handle your true nature yet.

MIKE

What about my false one?

    (*She smiles.*)

I met someone.

CANDY

Are you being careful? This "gay cancer" thing that's going around is very scary.

MIKE

Shut up about that. That's all anyone talks about now. Christ, we haven't even held hands yet.

CANDY

Liar. I know you guys go right to third base. You don't have to pretend with me.

MIKE

Hey, I waited a long time before coming out. I'm not going to let any of these friggin' Evangelicals scare me into thinking this is God's punishment for my pleasure.

CANDY

Keep your voice down, please. One haranguing male per hour is my limit.

MIKE

Sorry. It just infuriates me. Look at us. I'm angry and you're…

CANDY

Go ahead, say it. Battered. Want to sing a duet? (*Beat.*) I'm scared, Mike. I want children, but not with Phil. Not with that lineage.

MIKE

Candy…

CANDY

I mean it.

MIKE

Now you listen to me, lady. Did I ever tell you about my little brother, Tommy?

CANDY

The high school coach.

MIKE

He just teaches social studies now, but yeah, him. Did I?

CANDY

Just how proud of him you are.

MIKE

Yeah well I didn't always feel *proud* of him. I used to feel *bad* for him because he never had kids of his own. "He doesn't have much of a legacy, poor thing," I'd say to my father just to get him started. "That's right. At least you gave me grandchildren, Mike!" the Old Man would gloat. "What did Tommy ever give me? Gas!" Single people weren't worth a dime to Dad. But you know what? When our father dropped dead, who got up to speak at his funeral? Not me, his beloved first-born, his breeder. My barren little runt of a brother gets up. But he doesn't talk about himself, or the resentments he has every right to feel. No. No, he recites a long inventory of everything my father accomplished in his seventy-eight years. The ordinary and the not-so-ordinary. "This man, with only an eighth grade education, could recite 'Oh, Captain, My Captain' in its entirety…" Like that. And then, he recites it, tears streaming down his face. None of us can believe what we're hearing. Tommy, the worthless one? Father Fanelli had asked him to read something from scripture—but he recites this very personal, true account of who our father really was, and what his life really signified. This, from the son who never had kids. Do you know how proud I felt to be that kid's brother then? And how ashamed of myself, after all the competition and putting him down? Christ, the stupid mistakes that fill every one of our unforgivable lifetimes—

(*He sobs. With one hand still holding the compress on her*
bruise, she tries touching his face. He stops her, adamantly.)

You don't have to be a parent to be worth something. Okay? My kids drive me up a fucking tree.

(*He turns away and pulls himself together.*)

Now, are we trimming or cutting or adding highlights…?

(*She laughs.*)

What?

(*She laughs harder. He toughens.*)

C'mon, I'm running a business here, lady.

CANDY

Cut! Chop it all off!

(*As Mike slowly unfurls a cape and cuts Candy's hair, lights*
fade to a glow. Sound of Puccini's "Humming Chorus" fades

in. A long, wordless interlude ensues, Mike tenderly snipping until…lights fade. Mike slips off and Candy steps down to audience.)

CANDY

I left there that day with my hair short in back and long in front, so I could cover my bruise. I thought it looked awful, until someone stopped traffic, rolled down his car window and yelled, "Hey, Gigi. You look like Leslie Caron!" (*Touched.*) Hey, Gigi…so, I went home and walked out on Phil. It was best all around. Phil had his own wake-up call shortly thereafter. A few DUIs and jail time will do that. Cleaned up and left his dad's business behind. Ah, the dominoes, once they fall…

(*Sally appears up left, coffee to-go in hand.*)

He wound up remarrying, lots of kids, and my guess is the new wife is no pushover. She's a tank, that one. I've heard they're happy, but… (*Whispers.*) …I don't trust the source.

(*Indicates Sally, who exits in a huff. Candy shrugs.*)

I floated into real estate and did pretty well on my own. Ironic, isn't it? After so much time traveling the world, that I would make a career out of finding places for people to settle down. My conversation began to drift toward diminutives—from "The comparative pleasures of Positano and Marbella on the Costa del Sol…landscapes of such wonder!" to "The best choice in countertops: Corian or granite?" Ah, life. It's a real shrink-wrap. I remarried. Bobby. A realtor also. No, no kids. Housing boomed in the Reagan years, and the trickle down looked like a good plan for a while. Didn't it? I helped Mike and his new partner, George, find a rundown old Victorian which they did up splendidly. Well, a little garish for the area, what with the two tones of purple…

MIKE (off)

(*Yelling.*) LAVENDER AND PLUM!

CANDY

Right, on the *exterior* trim. He kept insisting the colors were "original, historic…"

MIKE (off)

"ARCHIVAL"! THE WORD IS "ARCHIVAL"!

CANDY

He was colorblind, for God's sake. The rest of the neighborhood was up in arms, but…he beautified that lot. For spite—and this is so typically Mike—he lined his driveway with a row of neo-classical nudes…

MIKE (off)

DAVIDS! MICHELANGELO'S DAVIDS! IF YOU'RE GOING TO TELL THE STORY, GET IT RIGHT!

CANDY

He faced them toward the neighbors and painted each a different shade of… (*She whispers.*) …lavender and plum. For a while I was a little embarrassed to show my face within a mile, but then we relocated down to the Cape. Me and Bobby McGee. No lie. Permanently. The North Shore. Brewster, to be exact. I lost touch with Mike for a few years. And then…and then there was the lump in my breast and the back and forth into Mass General. Uh-oh…I know what you're thinking. Here comes the Lifetime special: "The Chick's Last Wish," or some such thing.

(*Celine Dion song up. She yells to booth…*)

Stop it!

(*Back to us.*)

Not this chick's, anyway. One day—God, was it '97, '98?—I had to see an endocrinologist out in the Natick-Framingham area experimenting with a new chemotherapy and I thought, "Why don't I just drop by for a little 'top and tails' at the old salon? Surprise Mike." I put the pretty wig I'd bought—they sell them to cancer patients at a discount, you know, tell your sick friends—I put the wig on the front seat of my car and drove up to what used to be StarCutz. Originally Salon Élan. The sign now said "Hairistocracy" and to tell you the truth, it looked pretty chic. (*Sigh.*) Damn changes…they just keep making sure you don't get too comfortable with the things you're fond of…

179

Scene 6

(Lights change. Sound comes up of Enya's "Orinoco Flow."
Candy walks stage right to the reception area. It's April, '97.
The salon's decor is now very minimal/ modern—black and
white, geometric shapes, spare. She takes it in. The phone
rings twice, a machine picks up.)

MIKE (V.O.)

(Mellifluous.) "Hello. Hairistocracy is presently closed. Normal
hours are Tuesday through Saturday, from 9 a.m. to 6 p.m., and on
Thursday until 9 p.m. To make or change an appointment, or to leave
a message, leave your name and number. We'll call back. And
please, speak slowly and clearly. It's good manners."

(A loud beep.)

CUSTOMER (V.O.)

(Irritating.) "Oh, hi Mike. This is Moira Killarney. I know I'm
running about twenty-five minutes late. My wolfhound, Shanti,
swallowed one of Ashley's Polly Pockets and they're having to pump
his stomach. I'm at the Poochy Clinic in Holliston now waiting, and
I'm just distraught…"

(As Moira drones on, Michael enters from off left, drying his
hands. Dressed all in black—shirt, pants, shoes—he sports
very short hair on his balding (or gray) head. He speaks over

the incoming message, not recognizing Candy's back.)

MIKE

I'm sorry, we're not opened yet.

(*Candy turns and smiles. His jaw drops.*)

CANDY

I was going to surprise you but I think you lost more hair than me.

(*Alternative version: "But I think you're more gray than I am bald."*)

MIKE

Candy? Hold it a second...

(*He goes up to desk where Moira's message is still droning on.*)

CUSTOMER (V.O.)

"...the vet says it's going to cost us close to a thousand dollars, and with both kids in private school and the mortgage and the boat payments, I don't know how we're going to afford to keep Carmelita on six days a week, let alone start the renovations to the summer cottage on the Vineyard—"

(*Mike picks up the phone abruptly.*)

MIKE

Moira, get here when you can.

(*He hangs up, turns to hug Candy tight. She winces.*) Where have you been hiding yourself? I've missed you so much.

181

CANDY

Oh, shit, Mike. The Cape is another world.

MIKE

George and I were in Provincetown for a week last summer. I tried to look you up but—

CANDY

You did not.

MIKE

No, but I thought about it every day. (*Beat.*) Every other day. (*Beat.*) Twice. How's Bert?

CANDY

Bob is fine. He quit smoking and put on sixty pounds.

MIKE

I'm on the patch. George's starving me with a liquids-only diet. I pee all the time. (*He moves close and touches her cap.*) So what's this?

CANDY

Don't make me show you yet.

MIKE

(*He gets it.*) Your eyes have never been brighter.

CANDY

It's that kind of thing that makes you the most popular boy in class. (*Taking in the room.*) Track lighting, huh? I like the changes.

MIKE

Oh…I would clutter it up more, you know me, but you got to keep up with the times. And of course, now everybody and his brother considers himself a home design expert. Goddamn *Architectural Digest*. The days of individual expression are dead, Candy. Dead.

CANDY

How's the house?

MIKE

Sudbury? Wildly, flamboyantly rococo. (*Shrugs.*) I gotta let it out somewhere. Every time I pull into the driveway with more shopping bags George wants to kill me. You want some coffee or tea?

CANDY

I'm fine.

MIKE

Some water?

(*She shakes her head no.*)

You look pale. Come and sit.

CANDY

Don't baby me, Mike.

MIKE

I'm sorry.

(*She moves to his chair and sits, tired. He follows.*)

You've got to at least tell me what kind.

CANDY

Tit.

MIKE

Both?

CANDY

There's just one now.

MIKE

Okay.

CANDY

It only got to Stage Two. It never metastasized. They're pretty
certain they got it all. Let's talk about something else?

(*Michael tries to catch her eyes. She turns away.*)

It's just that you're getting that same stupid sympathy look that
everyone gets on their faces and I'm not having it. Not from you.

MIKE

(*Beat. Mock cheerful.*) How about them Celtics?

(*She can't help laughing.*)

CANDY

Get me some water, asshole.

MIKE

Please.

CANDY

No, no "please." That's the one privilege I've earned from this.
Unconditional courtesy.

(*He nods his assent, and goes off for water. She calls after.*)

How's *your* health?

MIKE

(*Returning.*) I never tested positive, if that's what you mean. (*Hands
her water.*)

CANDY

I'm glad. And thank you.

MIKE

Bite me. I'm lucky. George showed up just in time.

CANDY

You look good. I like the baldy. (*Alternatively, "gray."*) How're the
kids?

MIKE

All over the place. (*He pulls photos out from his station.*) Danny's
married with two kids in Santa Fe. Ginny's studying massage therapy
in New Hampshire. They're always pestering me to visit them, but—

CANDY

(*Finishing his thought.*) You hate kids.

MIKE

I hate *crossing state lines.*

CANDY

I nearly choked when you said you were on the Cape.

MIKE

We're actually thinking of relocating there.

CANDY

(*Swoony.*) Oh, Mike…I'd love to have you nearby.

MIKE

Listen to Miss Mood Swing. What have they got you on, acid?

CANDY

Don't get a swelled head. I'd just like access to a beautician who doesn't cater to the granny clientele.

MIKE

That's all I'd have to look forward to, isn't it? Blue rinses.

CANDY

And me! Shit, I almost forgot. Look in that bag… (*Points right.*) Please?

MIKE

(*As he crosses.*) That wasn't so hard. What's in it? CAKE?!

CANDY

Linzer tarts. Look in the small box.

(*He does.*)

Open it.

(*He does—a blonde wig.*)

You're the only one I trust to make it look like me.

MIKE

Aw, Candy. The color's perfect.

CANDY

It needs to be cut and set, I think. But it's good, no?

MIKE

It's good. (*He looks at her longingly, starts to tear up.*)

CANDY

Oh, now quit your bawling or I'll airlift that Moira woman out of her Poochy Clinic and sic her on you.

MIKE

Yikes! I'll start it right now. (*He carries the wig off left.*)

CANDY

(*Smiles to herself.*) Moira. What a funny name. There was a Moira at Miss Porter's. Moira…

MIKE (off)

What was her last name? Chenille? Chantilly?

CANDY

(*Laughing.*) *Something* Irish…

> (*Sally enters. Under Candy's gaze, she opens Mike's station*
> *drawer, brazenly takes two cigarettes from his pack and a*
> *five dollar bill. She exits with a smirk. Candy calls off.*)

MIKE! I THOUGHT YOU SAID YOU QUIT SMOKING!

MIKE (off)

GET OUT OF MY DRAWERS!

CANDY

MIKE!

MIKE (off)

IT'S JUST A BACKUP PACK! (*Going about his work.*) God, you can't beat human hair.

CANDY

DON'T CUT IT TOO SHORT! (*Concerned about Sally.*) Keep it classic.

MIKE (off)

Like Mary Martin in "Peter Pan"?

CANDY

NO! JULIE CHRISTIE IN "SHAMPOO." MIKE! PROMISE ME YOU'LL STOP SMOKING…

(*He sashays in wearing her wig.*)

TAKE THAT WIG OFF, YOU BASTARD!

(*They share a laugh as lights crossfade down. Candy steps down right, Mike left to style the wig. For the first time each seems to address the audience though in truth, only she does. Mike simply shares the scene.*)

CANDY	MIKE
How do you measure your life? The value of it.	
	Do you really want to go there?
Just ordinary Joes and Janes. Kids don't really dwell on it too much…	
	Why should they, when life stretches out infinitely?
…but I think just *people-*	
people? We're usually too	

CANDY	MIKE

CANDY

Busy making ends meet and
staying healthy and alive and
responsible and on time and
keeping in touch with the ones that
really matter to us…

MIKE

…and paying that stack of
bills, and who-gets-what-for-
Christmas…

CANDY

…to really measure things like
why life is valuable. We get
glimpses, that's it. A little
"Clarence" bell goes off in a
certain season…

MIKE

(*He chimes—ding!*)

CANDY

…or hearing a long-forgotten
tune…

MIKE

(*Sings a sentimental
tune.*)

CANDY

(*Stares at him.*)

MIKE

Yeah, even I'm susceptible to
mood swings.

CANDY

…but soon enough we're back to,
"Stay in your own lane, asshole!"
– or, "Get off the cellphone,
missy!"

189

CANDY	MIKE
	Or my personal favorite:
	(*Pretends to pick up a phone.*)
	"I'm about to sit down to dinner.
	How about you give me your
	HOME NUMBER and I'll call
	you back AT MIDNIGHT to
	discuss my mortgage rate?
	(*Slams down imaginary phone.*)
	–JESUS!"
(*She smiles.*) Passing the big	
divides—turning sixty-five,	
say, or surviving open heart	
surgery…	
	…or the miracle of remission—
(*She catches his glance.*)	
They're usually the little pit	
stops that force us to finally	
ask, "What difference have I	
made?" (*Looks back out.*) Sad,	
really. But right, somehow,	
too.	
	(*Mike slowly takes wig and exits.*)

CANDY

A tree doesn't ask how come, does it? It's just spring and then it's fall. The old dog just stops getting up…right, Mike? (*She looks around but he's gone.*) Mike…? The things we take for granted—because we must, mustn't we, otherwise we'd never get out of bed—well, we go on. Comrades fall, we step over the bodies. Which is very tricky, I have found, when you've been counting yourself among the wounded. (*Candy exits, as…*)

Scene 7

(2002—sound of a jetliner, loud and close. Music up: Bruce Springsteen's "The Rising." Mike enters from left, in jeans, vest, and sweatshirt, and moves down right. His posture and attitude indicate that he has aged noticeably. Sally is also noticeably older, her hair now streaked gray in a slightly-more-stylish-than-Buster-Brown cut, but still dressed as a wannabe-teen in a famous author T-shirt. As jet sound fades, Sally and Mike sit at reception desk folding foil, making supply lists, stocking shelves.)

SALLY

Oh, and order a case of Paul Mitchell's tea tree shampoo. They're flying off the shelves at Super Cuts.

MIKE

Fuckin' chains.

SALLY

Anyway, I really just don't get it. I mean, he's nice, but don't guys know by now that women hate it when they stare at our tits?

MIKE

Sally, you wear T-shirts with quotes on them. Maybe he just likes to read.

SALLY

No, Mike. I know the difference between a reader and a horndog.
This guy's a hound.

MIKE

Look, you're wearing a quote from some famous author right now.
Watch this…

(*His eyes travel back and forth across her chest, reading.*
Note: Quote could be one of Oscar Wilde's. He giggles.)
That's funny actually.

SALLY

Yeah, but your eyes moved.

MIKE

And your point would be?

SALLY

His don't.

MIKE

So he's hypnotized by mammaries. There are worse things.

SALLY

Like?

MIKE

Fisting.

SALLY

(*Beat.*) I don't even know what that is.

MIKE

Trust me, ignorance is bliss. (*A breath.*) You know, the real issue is you shouldn't be dating your son's guidance counselors.

SALLY

Clapton's okay with it.

MIKE

Clapton's a stoner, Sal.

SALLY

He's A.D.D.!

MIKE

Call it what you want, his pupils are dilated *all the time*. He's not of this earth. What does Hendrix think?

SALLY

Both my sons hate me anyhow.

MIKE

Honey, adolescence is a flu. They're gonna get over it. (*Appalled.*) Besides, you named them after rock stars! They should anoint you with the blood of all the nubile virgins who'll throw themselves at their unwashed feet.

SALLY

Finney named Hendrix, not me. He was so happy that night in the kitchen when I agreed to it, dancing all around pumping his air guitar. (*Beginning to tear up.*) He was such a good older brother… (*Her face in her hands.*)

194

MIKE

(*Beat.*) Finney died a hero, Sal.

SALLY

(*Nodding, inconsolable.*) It's almost a year. The boys want me to go
down to Ground Zero for the ceremony, but I can't, Mike. I can't. So
they hate me.

(*She dissolves. He takes her in his arms.*)

He was so excited to be training at Windows— (*She can't go on.*)

MIKE

Alright, Sally Starfish. Be brave. Be brave. I'll talk to your runts
when they get here. (*Rubbing her back.*) No one's been able to digest
this yet. It's too soon. All they need is a sense of completion around
their big brother's death. Don't you? (*He lifts her chin.*) I think
Mommy does.

SALLY

I can't.

MIKE

(*Backing off.*) Okay, so here's what you *can* do. It's dead today
anyway, and you don't want to be interviewed, right?—I can't
believe I let those two goofballs of yours talk me into this…a
documentary? On *me*? Who gives a shit about the hairdresser's life?
(*Hands her a tissue.*) So…go next door to the pharmacy and pick up
my prescription. Then take the afternoon. Hit the mall or something.

SALLY

(*Bucking up.*) *That* I can do. (*She starts to pull on her bangs in the mirror.*)

MIKE

And leave your bangs alone. They don't get longer by pulling. Go on! I got a half hour before Spielberg and Lucas get here and my stomach is burning. Vamoos!

SALLY

(*Hurrying off, she stops.*) You're a smartypants, mister. (*Sticks out tongue.*)

MIKE

And if I catch you coming out of Dunkin' Donuts with a bear claw in your bag I'm gonna tell the boys the truth about their fathers. ON CAMERA!

SALLY (off)

They know!

MIKE

(*Calling after.*) The village idiot part, or how they were conceived behind the dumpster in the trailer park?

> (*They "raspberry" each other. Sally's laughter can be heard offstage. Mike turns, a little ashen. He moves tentatively to his chair, a downstage spot, a slight limp apparent. Sits. He clips on a little lavelier mic.*)

Testing. Testing. (*Looks as if he's speaking to a camera.*) Good?

Good.

(*He pinches his cheeks, wets the tip of a finger, smoothes down his eyebrows, squares himself, and...*)

OFF-STAGE TEEN'S VOICE (pre-recorded)

You okay, Uncle Mikey?

(*Mike nods.*)

Okay...ACTION!

MIKE

(*To unseen camera, though really to audience.*) So, later that year I sold the business to your mom...sorry, Sally. And now, 2008, after my little hip replacement—noticeable, right?—and a few months of physical therapy—excruciating. Don't let anyone convince you otherwise—I'm back here. (*Askance.*) Framingham. I'm just renting this chair. I'm semi-retired, working three half-days a week these last six years. The following has dwindled, but...what am I going to do? Sit home, dusting knick-knacks? I guess I could try watercoloring. (*He bucks up, a little more of his old vigor.*) Anyway, I finally came to a tough decision. Not alone, mind you. George and I have decided it might be time to wander off to that sun-drenched peninsula we used to call "the elephants' burial ground"—Flor-ee-duh. Tell no one. (*Shrug.*) We have family there. Lana, Becky, Ginny...not friends, but family, and they are who we count on. They are how we measure *our* lives. Except, what I didn't take into account—I forgot to really, having stood behind a chair for nearly forty years combing

197

and curling and teasing and spraying and snip-snip-snip… "How's your back, Mrs. Klebanoff?" "Change conditioners, Donna?" "Sharon, I LOVE that tan!" I didn't think I could ever ask a customer—"Am I valuable? How would *you* measure my life?" It just seems… what's the word everybody uses now? No, not "offensive." (*Wrinkles brow.*) …damnit, what is that goddamned word?

> (*As he pinches the bridge of his nose, Sally moves on and sits behind desk, doing books. Candy, older too, enters in a shampoo cape, with…*)

CANDY

Inappropriate.

OFF-STAGE TEEN'S VOICE (pre-recorded)

And CUT! Okay, we got what we need. Thanks, Uncle M.

> (*Mike seems disoriented, both his real world and docu-world inexplicably overlapping. Finally, the real world shop presides as…*)

Scene 8

(Lights restore. Sound of some dreadfully schlocky Celine Dion song—"My Heart Will Go On"?—plays. Candy gives the booth a killer look...she nudges Mike out of his chair and sits in his place. It's 2008. The shop is now "Sally's Hair Apparent" and it's hopelessly unstylish.

Sally herself rises from behind the desk, in a curly gray wig, glasses, ugly sweatsuit and track shoes. She's grown, shall we say, broad in the beam? She's carrying a mug of coffee back to the sinks and she stops at Mike's station with her now-characteristic scowl.)

SALLY

Michael, I got to get that supply order in before eleven, so can you please not dawdle here over Princess Leia? *(Of Candy, defensively.)*
(They glare at her as she wanders off right.)

CANDY

(Beat.) Inappropriate.

MIKE

(Startled, putting on glasses.) What?

CANDY

(Enunciating.) The word you're looking for is in-ap-pro-pri-ate.

MIKE

What word?

CANDY

Oh, Jesus, Mike. It's bad enough you drag me to this mortuary every month. Don't make matters worse by losing your memory. ADJUST YOUR HEARING AID! And get out of that damn sweater. You've been wearing the same one for years.

MIKE

(*Pretending dementia.*) WHO ARE YOU?! Are you my mommy?

>(*They both snigger, but something's off. They grow quiet for a few moments of silence as Mike begins his prep work, disinterested, with Candy handing him the occasional roller or clip. Sound of the Celine Dion song segues into something even more insidious…her "Beauty and the Beast"?*

>*More silence. Mike's lethargy is palpable. He even pauses mid-gesture now and then to stare into space. Finally…*)

CANDY

What's with you today?

MIKE

What do you mean?

CANDY

Don't answer my question with a question.

MIKE

(*He shrugs.*) I don't know what you're talking about.

CANDY

(*Changing subject, exasperated.*) So, anyway, L.A…you can have it.
I'm not going back…where else in the world would they build an art
museum over a tar pit? Wait 'til you hear this…

MIKE

Keep it short, darling, or I lose the will to live.

(*Candy smacks him and proceeds to riff on L.A.*)

CANDY

So they're all terrified, right? About this economy thing. Like the rest
of us are rolling in clover. But you want to measure the level of
people's stress? Monitor their driving habits. Changing lanes without
signaling's got to be the third cause for a homicidal rampage behind
long lines at the post office and a delayed plane on the tarmac…you
think Bostonians are bad? We got stuck on Sunset in Brentwood
for—

(*He turns her chair upstage as Candy freezes in the gesture of
prattling on. Mike, his comb in the air, his arm freezing there,
turns to the audience as if he's still speaking to the
"camera."*)

MIKE

And as she buckled her seatbelt to continue her Michelin pan of Los
Angeles, I took a detour through an unexpectedly scenic route. I

don't know what came over me that day…

(*Lights begin to change.*)

…I found myself imagining what it would have been like, all those years ago, had I been straight. I mean, really straight, not camouflaged to appear so, but honestly and thoroughly heterosexual…standing here, behind this chair, when this lovely, luminous, flawed little bird with a broken wing came sputtering out of the sky into my shop…what would I have done? Would I have appreciated the special air of self-importance and pride she flaunted like a birthright? Or would I have charged like a horny bull toward a red cape? (*He laughs to himself.*) What if I had been straight?

(*Sound of lush music—Sinatra. Mike lifts Candy out of his chair. They dance together to "I've Got You Under My Skin" romantically, like a young couple very much in love:*

"I would sacrifice anything, come what might for the sake of having you near, In spite of a warning voice that comes in the night and repeats and repeats in my ear…"

Music builds and builds as they whirl about the stage, everything disappearing but Mike and Candy, dancing beneath a blanket of stars, until…he puts her back in the chair and sound fades.

202

*Lights restore, Candy resuming her seat and continuing her
L.A. rant for real, and Mike, in a daze, stands off to one side,
his comb in the air.*)

CANDY

…but Bobby's sister, Fran—I told you about Fran. She's the V.P at
Sony—God help the Japanese! She's out there kvelling about Culver
City this and Brentwood that, but I've seen enough, I'll tell ya. I
don't need to go back. She had her assistant blow up the *air mattress*
for us in her home office and then spends the whole week
complaining she can't get to her desk. This from a woman who had
steel joists installed under her kitchen floor for the thousand pound
Viking stove, and she doesn't cook! We eat out every night. Not
cheap. If it isn't the A.O.C. or the B.L.D. or the S.L.S.—oh, this is
the latest thing out there. Acronyms. We spent a hundred and sixty
dollars on grilled cheese sandwiches that I'm still digesting. I'm
telling you, you can have it. I'm done.

(*Michael, pale, his comb shaking, puts down his arm.*)
What is wrong with you? Did you change anti-depressants?

MIKE

(*Dissembling, a rage building.*) Did you watch the Academy
Awards?

CANDY

Bob had it on but I couldn't. I went into the other room to watch that
Capote movie.

MIKE

(*Back to old self.*) The dreary one or the fun one?

CANDY

One of them is fun? The one with What's-His-Name? Who's in everything? (*Beat.*) He just won the Oscar…

MIKE

Who was your first husband?

CANDY

Phil? (*Realizing.*) Oh, Phillip Seymour Hoffman!

MIKE

That's the one I won't see. I'm too upset about *Brokeback Mountain*.

CANDY

You wha-what…? What's one got to do with the other?

(*Her cellphone rings—a jarring ringtone.*)

Give me my bag.

(*He does. She finds phone and answers.*)

CANDY	MIKE
…what? No, I'm still in the chair…yeah, well it takes him a little longer now…oh shit, honey, I completely forgot…! What? I'm sorry, you're breaking up… (*She gets up and walks a few paces away.*) The market what? Our portfolio…? Oh, God. Yes, I	(*Like a dog with a bone.*) A little thing called THE OSCARS? You must know those. They hold them at the Moose Lodge in the backwoods of Ontario when the moon is full. For a cabal of toothless goat herders? There's a ritual sacrifice…and a little fish

204

CANDY	MIKE
will, as soon as I get out of	stick dance…perhaps you've
here…okay…okay, bye. (*Off*	seen the smoke signals?
phone, to Mike.) What?	

(*Beat.*)

CANDY

What are you, having a stroke? (*Putting phone in bag as she sits.*)
Can we finish up, please? I gotta pick Bobby up at the Club.

(*He doesn't move.*)

Hey, Rip Van Winkle, wake up!

MIKE

(*Angering.*) That beautiful boy, Heath Ledger, deserved to win this
year. And the forgettable *Crash* is *not* Best Picture. (*He furiously
cleans his comb, under his breath.*) I happen to have a dozen of these
sweaters, for your information.

CANDY

(*Baffled.*) You used to have a talent for loose associations.

MIKE

Brokeback Mountain should have gotten Best Picture!

CANDY

Ooof…don't be stupid. Too much yearning.

(*He stops working.*)

So sue me, I don't like stories about yearning. Can you speed it up?

(*He swivels her chair in the direction of the exit, stage right.*)

MIKE

Get out of my chair.

CANDY

(*Amused.*) What are you doing?

MIKE

We can't be friends anymore.

CANDY

Why? Cause I didn't like—?

MIKE

DON'T…even utter the title. You're not worthy.

CANDY

You've got dementia.

MIKE

I'm serious. Get the hell out. (*He flings her bag.*)

CANDY

(*Getting up.*) Fine. (*Angry, getting out of her cape.*) You and your stupid gender politics. *Brokeback Mountain* BORED ME…and it bored my straight husband, Bob, too. So there! So does Judy Garland, for *your information. And* Barbra Streisand—

MIKE

Who listens to her anymore? I don't listen to Barbra Streisand—

CANDY

WHEN SHE WAS YOUNG?! (*She storms off, then back on.*) And after all these years, you know what? So do YOU! You bore me,

Michael, because you're all the same. You're victims, you gays. Even when you're winning and the world says, "Go ahead. Be and do whatever the hell you want to be and do. Take over." Who cares? Shake your saggy gay booty down the middle of Commonwealth Avenue. WE DON'T CARE! Marry each other and adopt infants from Romania and increase the value of rundown properties with your high-toned tastes and Marimeekko drapes—

MIKE

(*Correcting her.*) Marimekko. (*Glib, he lights a cigarette.*)

(*Candy picks up his hand mirror and smashes it. Note: For production ease, she may spill his roller tray instead. As she gathers her things, Mike picks up his cane and begins to slowly make his way off. She reaches in her purse.*)

CANDY

I'll leave money for your services on your station…watch out "The Girl" doesn't take it.

MIKE

(*Quietly, over his shoulder.*) Her name is Sally.

CANDY

(*Calling after.*) Did you hear me?

(*He's gone.*)

Fine. Sulk. I've had it! There are plenty of good hairdressers out there. (*She starts off, stops, turns for one last parry.*) And cross me off the book for next week, too!

(*Candy turns out to audience, stricken by her own fury.*)
And I guess that's what he did. I don't know, I stopped going. I don't know why I got so mad. Maybe I just resented the intimacy. How do you sustain that? For so long? (*Exits.*)

(*Sally, having heard the conflagration, returns, a crappy gingham curtain in one hand, a dustpan in the other. She sees the mess.*)

SALLY

(*To audience.*) Oh, for God's sake, how much cleaning can one person bear?

(*She turns on some music—Amy Winehouse's cover of "Our Day Will Come"—and begins to adjust various elements of the shop until its transformation into the dreaded "granny" shop is complete. She calls off instructions to her new shampoo girl.*)

So listen, Tiffany…I know it's your first day, but after you finish shampooing Cho-Cho San, I want you out in front of the shop passing out discount coupons. You can slip 'em under the wipers on parked cars, staple some on poles—but don't wise off if people harass you. We don't want to alienate a soul. Once they're in, remember this: "The customer's approval makes all the labor worthwhile." Beauty etiquette.

(*Candy returns, restored to her opening look from top of play, stands off to one side to observe. Lights crossfade back to*

Candy's spot.)

CANDY

I stayed away for a few months—okay, more than a few. I hated what that shop had become. "Just Sally's." No style at all. In that stupid little strip mall between Mail Boxes Etc. and Big Lots? Ick. The only reason I had kept going there was Mike. Anyway, I found a trendy little day spa in Chatham run by some fresh kids from the Lower East Side…real *artistes*. Cerisse and Orphée… adorable. Great haircutters. I felt vital again. It showed. Even Bob noticed. Last month, I happened to have a meeting in Framingham with a sponsor for Relay for Life—they raise money for cancer research, great folks—and out of curiosity…well, I was right there. "Just Sally's"…so I poked my head in just to say hi. I mean, c'mon. It was all nonsense. We were old friends, Mike and I. And then I got an earful…

(*Candy enters shop. Sally picks up a bag of hair while on cellphone.*)

Scene 9

SALLY

…okay, gotcha. Yeah, I got it right here. Bye.

(*She hangs up. They face off.*)

They're collecting hair for the Gulf. They say it absorbs oil.

CANDY

I heard that on NPR.

(*Beat. They stand awkwardly appraising each other.*)

SALLY

Mike's not here.

CANDY

Okay. (*She turns to go.*)

SALLY

Did you want to make an appointment?

CANDY

Oh…no, not really.

SALLY

Right.

(*Beat. They stare at each other.*)

You know, I never liked you.

CANDY

I'm sorry.

SALLY

Well I don't think there was ever any love lost either way, do you?

(*Candy just smiles. Beat.*)

CANDY

Where is Mike? Just out of curiosity.

SALLY

Florida. He and George got a condo in Naples.

CANDY

(*Musing.*) They really did it. It's nice there. You hear from them much?

SALLY

Christmas cards. The occasional thank you whenever I send him a check...for what's still owed.

CANDY

Owed? On the business, or a loan?

SALLY

(*Sally smirks, looks out window.*) That your Mercedes?

(*Candy nods.*)

I drive that dinged up Yaris, plastic piece o' shit. Well, I'm paying off a big debt, so...don't suppose you have to worry about carrying any bank notes. (*Sally appraises her—can she be trusted?*) Let me spell something out for you. My big secret—how someone like me survives: stealing. I stole.

(*Candy's taken aback.*)

… from Mike. (*Laughs.*) You were expecting me to say, "I went to law school?" No, Candy, I stole, plain and simple. And he let me get away with it for nearly fifteen years. He knew. Fucker. (*She studies Candy.*) Makes you uncomfortable, doesn't it? You would never do something like that, would you? Steal from a friend, let alone allow them to get away with it. Then again, I wouldn't walk out on a friend like Mike for all the Bavarian motorcars in the world, so maybe we're even. I guess you never had a meth habit, or three kids out of wedlock, or… (*With great irony.*) But in case you do some day, and your survival requires desperate measures, here's two cents from the horse's mouth. Choose the right guy to steal from. Mike never held it against me. He knew, but he kept his mouth shut. And don't think for one second I didn't want to get caught. It got so that I began to suspect he was *letting* me get away with it, so I made it a little more obvious. Every time he'd catch another discrepancy in the books, he turned a blind eye. Do you know how hard that is to live with? (*Almost loses it, but quickly recovering.*) Anyway, I put three kids through college and the baby's just graduating from State. Not bad for a fuck-up like me. But you know—in the end? I didn't do it all alone. We did it, me and that… (*She leans on the word.*) …*hairdresser*. No, honey. You can bet your sweet ass I'd never walk away from someone like that without paying back my debt. I know what a friend is worth. (*Goes to the desk, holds up a deposit bag.*) Right here. Ten percent of anything I make now goes into this account. Should the time come… (*She chokes back a sob.*) Mike will have a little cushion… (*Sally turns away.*) You better put money in your meter. The town's going broke and that meter maid's got a quota.

CANDY

(*Starts to leave, pauses.*) Thanks for telling me all that, Sal.

SALLY

(*Sally nods, recovers.*) I'm thinking about putting in WiFi and a cappuccino machine. What do you think?

> (*Takes the gingham curtain and struggles to hold it above a window. Candy simply and graciously lends her a hand, but the fabric looks like shit and they both know it.*)

Aw crap, he'd kill me if he saw me hang gingham.

> (*She rolls the curtain in a ball, begins to exit. Candy touches Mike's chair. In afterthought, Sally retrieves a postcard from Mike's station.*)

This came about a month ago.

> (*She hands it to Candy and exits. Candy dons reading glasses, reads.*)

MIKE (V.O.)

"Florida just delightful, Sal. Muggy, buggy, and slow-moving elephants lined up for their goddamn early bird specials. Can you picture yours truly gumming stewed prunes? Yuck. God, I miss my chair! Love, Mike. P.S. Ever hear from Candy?"

> (*She lovingly puts card on Mike's chair, takes off glasses,*)

213

steps downstage to audience.)

CANDY

And then, out of the blue, Sally was kind enough to phone when she got the call from George…Mike died. Mike died? (*Very long beat.*) I don't know if enough can be said about friendship.

EPILOGUE

(Candy is back in her special spot down left as at top.)

It's May now on the Cape. Don't get your hopes up. It's winter by anyplace else's standards. Mike's family couldn't all get together for his funeral. It happened so abruptly and they're really spread out now. I spoke to George the other day who called to let me know that they're all coming in this weekend for a memorial service in P-Town…Mike always loved Provincetown. The truth is, he wasn't that fond of the Cape really, but P-Town was something else. Well, it is, isn't it? He said they're going to spread his ashes on the gay beach there…aren't all the beaches gay there? What's it called? Herring Bone Cove? No…Herring Cove Beach! So happens that I'm scheduled for a knee replacement, so I don't think…who'd know me? I'd feel awkward. You know? What's the word? Inappropriate? Who am I, after all? *(She catches her breath mid-sob.)* Who am I? *(After a beat, she pulls herself together.)* Alright, look…let me end this before it gets—

(Cue Celine Dion.)

Are you *kidding*? NO!

(Cue stops. Clearing her throat, she reaches into her pocket and takes out a small Moleskine notebook.)

So I'm *not* going to Mike's memorial today, okay? But, here, now, on my own… (*Deep breath in.*) I can do this, I can do this…

> (*And long exhalation. Ready, formal now, she takes a step further downstage.*)

I would like to commemorate someone I knew for a long time who helped me at a few critical junctures in my life…just a friend, really. A really, really, *really* good friend. I think he'd appreciate this… (*Indicating book.*) Well, he liked his lists. It isn't "O Captain! My Captain!" but…so, here we go.

> (*She opens the notebook, reads, eventually just reciting.*)

A curling iron. A rattail comb. A styling fork. Curlers.

Perm solution and cap.

A pack of Salems.

Coffee, light with Cremora and three sugars,

Linzer tarts for dipping in the coffee. And cake. He *was* cake.

Roux Rinses,

Clairol Coloring Kits,

Ozone Hairspray in the pink and gray can—it really was called "Ozone," can you imagine! Well, what did he know about fluorocarbons? Or care?

Hair clips, Scissors, Movies, Heath Ledger, who was, I can now admit, pretty wonderful.

Music, all kinds, cutting edge to classical, Bach to Sarah Vaughn…the soundtrack of a life…his life.

Fashion, yes *fashion*. From high to low to lower, but always with a flare. Including Pirate Shirts, Go-Go Boots, Rings, Extensions, Frownies, Falsies, Ziggy pants, and toward the end, bless his heart, the occasional and well-concealed Depends. There's an art to that, trust me. Oh, and Art. Ah, Art, with a capital A—his little closet obsession. His *raison d'etre*! His parents were right, he should have stayed in art school. Instead he made a masterpiece of tangles every half hour for forty years. My Michelangelo.

Behind a chair, in front of a mirror…standing and staring and dancing all day.

Dancing! "The worst loss of all social arts," he'd say. My God, could my Mike hustle…

> (*As Candy continues with her litany of things, the lights begin to swell on the rest of the stage and sound of elegiac music grows.*
>
> *Mike, dressed as he was when we first met him, appears from off left dancing, with a cup of coffee and tiara box. The set transforms to something akin to what we first saw in Scene 1. Mike preparing his station for a day's work. The sound of voices, a busy shop.*)

Brushing and teasing—teasing, both senses. Tanning all summer 'til shoe-leather dry.

The color purple—not the movie or book, the *color*, in all its invincibly sexy shades.

217

The contradictions and the loyalties. Sally…

(*Young Sally enters, crosses to desk, sits.*)

His absolute refusal to travel far from home.

His ex-wife, Becky, checked in on every Sunday,

His family…sister, brother, those always-irksome kids…

Still, family, no matter how big a pain in the ass…family. Don't squirm, you're lucky if you have them.

And if you got a George, the one constant, who in the end will be the one to make all the calls…

(*Candy's litany accelerates, grows more urgent.*)

Being of your time, taking time, listening, stopping…

To look, to see, to know—and this is no small trick Mike had going—

(*All through this, Mike is busy at his station, carefully placing the tiara box down, while Sally works at the reception desk.*)

To know how to match a skin tone, how to translate a trend into a style you can live with, how to disguise a flaw, a blemish, a wound, the damages of aging—split ends, disintegrating sheen—how to frame a face, face after face after face—my face…year after year after…

(*Breaking off. Tenderly, Mike opens the box he's holding and lifts out her bridal tiara from the "wedding day" scene. He slowly crosses to where she stands.*)

And last…I guess *least*, which has always been my downfall… how to boost the confidence of someone so uncertain…a girl who needs approval…

MIKE

(*Out of the shadows, he hands her the tiara.*) Candy?

CANDY

(*To audience, with a simple shrug.*) …me.

(*She puts the tiara on, as…lights fade to black.*)

END OF PLAY.

Author's Note:

For all the girlfriends—
you know who you are—
And for Mike,
Who taught me the steps.

-T. A.

IV. COMMITMENT'S SABOTEURS

FOREVER HOUSE

<u>Characters:</u>
BEN EVANS AND JACK McINTYRE — a gay couple, mid-30s.
GLORIA CHALMERS* — a neighborhood busybody, 30-50.
BILL DIMMELWICH* — a realtor, 50-65.
EVELYN GROSSMAN — Jack's Jewish mother, around 60.
PETE AND FRANCINE LEFONTIERE* — the Evangelicals next door; he 50s, she 40.

Actress playing Gloria may double Francine, Bill may double Pete.

In addition, various voices such as of the mayor or figments of Jack's imagination may be realized through sound or projection effects. Or a director may find other creative methods to good effect.

<u>Setting:</u>
A vintage craftsman bungalow in Earthly Delights, an upscale suburban enclave of such houses built around 1910 just outside Los Angeles, CA. The time is the present, sometime within the first decades of the 2000s, and one year later.

Act I—a bare living room with upstage staircase separated by arch, a door to the basement inset beneath the stairs.

Act II—a nearly empty basement child's nursery with upstage stairs. Rooms configured the same in both acts.

Author's note: End of line slashes "//" signify dialogue overlaps.

Production History:

A reading of *FOREVER HOUSE* was first presented as part of the Skylight Theatre Company's INKubator series in 2013 under the direction of Elizabeth Swain and starring Ryland Shelton, John Lavelle, Dale Raoul, Eve Gordon and Michael Kearns, with stage directions read by Rebekah Tripp.

The full production had its world premiere at the Skylight Theatre in 2015, produced by Gary Grossman, directed by Elizabeth Swain, and assisted by Rachel Berney Needleman, starring James Liebman, Michael Rubenstone, Dale Raoul, Elyse Mirto (understudied by Jane Petrov), and Joel Swetow, with set designed by John Iacovelli, costumes by Terri Lewis, lights by Jeff McLaughlin, sound by Peter Bayne, projections by Nick Santiago, and staged managed by Christopher Hoffman.

FOREVER HOUSE
Dale Raoul (Evelyn), Michael Rubenstone (Jack) & James Liebman (Ben)

Elyse Mirto (Francine), Joel Swetow (Pete), James Liebman (Ben) &
Michael Rubenstone (Jack), Skylight Theatre
PHOTOS: ED KRIEGER

"There is a great deal of pity and tenderness in all of us, but when a certain balance is broken by things that create exhaustion…the underground devils come out—which makes for naked and savage kinds of creation."

-Tennessee Williams

We shape our self
to fit this world
and by the world
are shaped again
The visible
And the invisible
Working together
In common cause,
To produce
The miraculous

-David Whyte
from "Working Together"

"Perhaps everything that frightens us is, in its deepest essence, something helpless that wants our love."

-Rainer Maria Rilke

ACT I

Prologue

(*A projection—travelogue-style footage of Southern California neighborhoods, vintage craftsman houses. Realtor's commercial begins in V.O.*)

BILL DIMMELWICH (V.O.)

Welcome to Earthly Delights, a newly restored enclave of *vintage* craftsman bungalows in the heart of sun-drenched Southern California, just thirty minutes northeast of Los Angeles. This bedroom community now thrives thanks to well-maintained freeway access, strong public schools and upscale amenities of every stripe! If you're an innovative, industrious young professional, take a virtual tour through any of our remaining properties. Experience tradition-bound luxury at *affordable* prices. Whether you're starting out, starting up, or just plain star-struck, you'll find your piece of heaven at Earthly Delights.

(*We see realtor Bill Dimmelwich now on screen.*)

Contact me, Bill Dimmelwich, your exclusive property representative, today: www.earthlydelights.com. Domestic craftsmanship elevated to fine art.

(*And the projection sputters out, crossfading...*)

<u>Scene 1</u>

(*Lights up on a completely empty, recently uncarpeted living room. Benjamin Britten's* Young Person's Guide to the Orchestra *plays from a small practical speaker as the real sound of carpet being torn up is heard, continuous.*

An archway upstage center leads to an empty, carpeted hallway with visible staircase and a door to the basement beneath. Within the downstage room, windows stage right reveal or suggest a garden with mature foliage, and tall glass doors stage left lead out to an arbor-covered patio. Above the arch sits a small stepladder, iPod, and speaker.

It is spring. Late afternoon. As the sound of carpet tearing continues, we see first the work boots and jean-clad legs of a man on his knees backing into view upstage right of the arch, progressing little by little into view, pulling up the rug.

This is BEN EVANS. *He is perhaps just 35—physically fit, masculine and nice looking. He wears a T-shirt and is sweaty.*

As he reaches mid-arch, Ben sits back on his haunches, winded, and wipes the sweat off his face with the tail of his T-

shirt. Beat. He stands, both hands on the piece of carpet
already peeled back, and with a ferocious growl, rips the rest
of the carpet up.)

BEN

AAARGHH! (*Mission accomplished.*) Arrivederci, fucker.

(*Ben carries the carpet fragments out the stage left door.*
Note: Throughout the following scene, Ben and Jack cross
back and forth, missing each other nearly every time.
Off up right, sound of front door opening—then voice of Jack,
mid-conversation on his cellphone.

Simultaneously, a light comes up on Jack's mother, EVELYN
GROSSMAN, *extreme stage left, home in her Florida condo*
on her cellphone to her son, perhaps doing her nails or
trimming a bonsai. She wears a caftan and speaks loudly,
awkward with her modern device.)

EVELYN

Just saying, in stressful situations you tend to mask your feelings…

JACK (off)

…I do NOT mask my feelings, Ma. Hold on a sec, I'm just walking in…

(*Enter* JACK McINTYRE, *mid-30s. An elegant suit; laptop*
case on shoulder; champagne bottle; in one hand, a large

Bed Bath & Beyond bag. He's on his iPhone, earbuds in,
taking it all in, putting things down.)

(*Calls.*) BENNY? (*On phone.*) Oh my God, you won't believe it,
he's ripped the shitty shag out already…

EVELYN

We didn't put shag in.

JACK

Of course you didn't, you and Dad were too tasteful for shag.

EVELYN

That's right. You come from people with good taste.

JACK

Thank you, Mommy. I love our gene pool, too…

EVELYN

What's that music?

JACK

(*On phone.*) Wait, let me shut it off… (*As he clicks off music.*) It's
Britten, Ma. Britten…

EVELYN

BRITNEY?

JACK

Not Britney, *Britten*, Benjamin—hold on… (*Calling.*) BENNY? YO!
(*Sniffs.*) YOU BURNING SOMETHING? (*Looking about.*) Where
the hell—? (*Crossing to open basement door.*) Ben? You down
there? (*No answer. He shuts basement door quickly.*) I don't know

why but that basement gives me the total heebie-jeebies…

                              EVELYN

Is it finished? Your father kept his workshop down there. I wish I

could see.

                              JACK

Well, if you'd learn how to FaceTime you could…

                              EVELYN

FaceTime, Facebook…I miss Polaroids.

                              JACK

Don't take umbrage with technology, Ma, it's a sure sign of aging,

like liver spots…

                              EVELYN

You got eyes, *describe* it.

                              JACK

Oh, you want the *audio* tour? Alright, here we are in the living room.

(*Taking in the expanse of the room.*) It's huge…

        (*He heads up right to retrieve a five-gallon primer can he left

        outside the front door.*)

                              EVELYN

They had space in California back then. I loved all the space.

                              JACK

I know, but since you were raised by wolves in the caves of Canarsie

I figured you were exaggerating… (*Sets can down stage right.*)

We're going to have her flocked wallpaper stripped—Ben calls it

                                231

"early Tim Burton"…

EVELYN

Lots of light still?

JACK

Windows on three sides, east, west, and south, yep…

EVELYN

See if the lemon bush we planted off the patio is still there.

JACK

(*Of stage left view.*) Lemon? What lemon…? (*Spotting it.*) Oh, yeah.
Not a bush anymore. (*Squints.*) It's a tree now, twelve feet…

EVELYN

(*Welling up.*) Oh my God…

JACK

Ma, don't cry, you'll ruin your mascara…

EVELYN

Are there rats?

JACK

Rats? What rats?

EVELYN

Rats love citrus. They're fruitarian. You see any, you gotta call the
exterminator quick.

JACK

We just closed, I'm not calling an exterminator…

(*As he makes one more trip to bring in a five-gallon can of spackle.*)

EVELYN

Don't be stupid. It's preemptive!

JACK

It's toxic!

EVELYN

When I was growing up we exterminated every month.

JACK

Sure, in New York, we had to, which is probably why our family is riddled with birth defects… (*Sets second can down right and sits on it.*)

EVELYN

What are you talkin'…?

JACK

Cousin Walter's misshapen head, my *allergies*…

EVELYN

You're excessively paranoid.

JACK

You bet I'm excessively paranoid, I'm thirty-five years old and I still seek my Mother's approval…

EVELYN

(*Shouting into the line.*) I'M GIVING YOU TIPS FOR SURVIVAL!

JACK

Ma, don't hock me a chainik…

EVELYN

(*Beat, restraining herself.*) Moving men there?

JACK

No, they delivered the beds this morning, the rest comes tomorrow…

EVELYN

(*Sigh.*) I'm happy for you, Jacky. You're making good choices. Grandchildren would be nice, but…I guess it all ends with you.

JACK

Ma, enough with the end-of-the-line talk. Not every couple procreates. Our DNA has seen its day.

(*Beat as Evelyn stews silently, unwilling to comment.*)

Hello? You there? …you're insulted.

EVELYN

(*Lying.*) I'm defrosting something.

JACK

Oh, I thought… (*Sound of door, off left.*) Hold on. (*Off phone, checking kitchen.*) BEN, IS THAT YOU?

(*Ben enters garden door left and goes upstairs, singing in falsetto.*)

BEN

"Working my way back to you, babe, with a burning love inside…"

(*Jack re-enters.*)

EVELYN

Again with the music?

JACK

(*Back on cell.*) No, we hired Frankie Valli to clear brush… (*Silent beat.*) I'm *kidding!* I'm gonna go…I'll call you tonight.

EVELYN

The girls are coming over.

JACK

Again with the Mahjong? Say hi to Mrs. Gunderschmitt…

EVELYN

She's back, poor thing. They took out a tumor the size of a grapefruit.

JACK

A grapefruit? Well, it's good she had it removed…

EVELYN

I'm sending you some of your grandmother's drapes.

JACK

Please, don't! Not till we choose the wall color…

EVELYN

They're packed already, along with the Goya.

JACK

Ma, keep the Goya print, that thing gave me nightmares all through grade school…

EVELYN

"Tales from the Crypt" did that. Don't blame Goya.

The print is called "The Sleep of Reason" for a reason— (*Faking it.*) Sorry, you're breaking up— (*Not.*) —More soon, BYE! (*He disconnects.*)

(*Light fades on an exasperated Evelyn. With a huge sigh of relief, Jack stands for moment, taking in the empty house. Joyful now, he closes his eyes, clicks his heels three times.*)
(*Apprehensively.*) "There's no place like home…there's no place like home…there's no place like home…"

(*Looks to the boom box—an inspiration. Switches to radio, a beat-heavy contemporary tune—White Stripes' "Fell in Love with a Girl"? Jack begins a spastic little dance. He positions himself center, drops trousers, puts champagne bottle between his legs and turns upstage toward the arch provocatively as Ben enters, beams, clicks off music, turns down toward Jack…*)

BEN

The neighbors are home.

JACK

Left or right? (*Ben points stage left.*) The Evangelicals? C'mon… let's give them a good eyeful. (*Still facing upstage, he lifts his front shirt tails and wiggles his hips.*)

BEN

What's that between your legs? Christ, Cristal? You bought Cristal?

JACK

Hey, I got your Cristal right here! (*Wiggles harder.*)

BEN

You actually splurged on a $600 bottle of champagne?

JACK

$635, baby! It's closing day. Come and get it!

GLORIA

(*From offstage right.*) Helloooo!

> (*Jack quickly pulls his pants up, scurries off through garden door left while Ben crosses up right, to meet, greet and distract at front door.*)

BEN (off)

Hi, how are you? What can I help you with?//

GLORIA (overlapping)

Hello, welcome! I hope I'm not…I'm Gloria Chalmers. I saw your cars in the driveway and just thought I'd drop off a little something.

> (*Ben escorts GLORIA CHALMERS, a housewife, late 30s, into the living room, stepping over Jack's stuff. She has a pastry box.*)

BEN

Watch your step here—//

> (*She sweeps down through the room.*)

GLORIA

(*Kvelling.*) Ooh, I just love an empty craftsman. And will you look at that floor! Doreen was always so proud of her Zhuo Zhuo Dong Chen shag, but you know, for the number of times a day she vacuumed it always looked dirty. Well... (*Shrugs.*) Kids and dogs. (*Nosing.*) That color is…vibrant.

BEN

We're still experimenting.

GLORIA

You and…?

JACK

(*Re-emerging, fully put together.*) Hello, I'm Jack.

> (*Gloria extends her hand. While shaking, there is an awkward pause during which Gloria appraises the situation, looking back and forth between the two men.*)

BEN

(*Of the pastry box.*) Can I help you with…?

GLORIA

Oh, of course! They're for you.

> (*Flirtatiously, she hands Ben the pastries, which he takes off to the kitchen.*)

A little welcome-to-the-neighborhood. La-la!

JACK

How sweet.

GLORIA

Bear claws? They are…sweet. (*Extending hand.*) Glo Chalmers.

238

(*They shake but she's looking after Ben.*) Our contractor likes them, so…I just…

JACK

Ben loves them, but he's got the metabolism. I gain weight just thinking—//

GLORIA

Is Ben…*your* contractor?

BEN

(*Re-entering.*) No, I'm… (*Trails off, looking to Jack.*)

JACK

Ben. He's Ben. (*Taps chest.*) I'm Jack. (*Off her look.*) We just closed. On the house. I was born here. Well, not *here* here. We lived here a bit…not we, my parents and I…in the late seventies. (*Spilling quickly.*) My father was a graphic designer for Condé Nast in New York, got transferred west when my mother was pregnant with me. Dad had a bad heart, Mom and I moved back east after he died, I was two, blah-blah-blah-blah-blah, listen to me—TMI! Anyway, we…no… (*Looks to Ben—should we do this?*) Ben?

BEN

We bought the house together. Their old house. We're, you know, partners.

GLORIA

(*Suspicions confirmed.*) Ah. Business or…what do you call that other way?

239

JACK

"Fuck buddies?"

BEN

Jack! Domestic partners.

GLORIA

THAT'S it! I always liked the formality of that phrase.

JACK

Me, too. Anything that starts with domestic. "Domestic help,"
"domestic squabbles…"

GLORIA

No, the *partners* part, silly. I think anything that stresses partnership
has a friendly ring. But that's me—old accentuate-the-positive Glo.
By the way, I'm president of the Earthly Delights Homeowners'
Coalition so in case you need any—

JACK

Coalescing?

BEN

Jack, let her finish.

GLORIA

It's okay, I get it. He's the funny one and you're the…*handy* one.

JACK

(*To Ben.*) She wanted to say "the straight man." (*To Gloria.*) Didn't
you? Admit it, you did, didn't you?

BEN

Jack! (*To her.*) Continue, please.

GLORIA

Thank you, I will. Just thought you should know we've had some issues lately here at Earthly Delights with outside elements coming over from adjacent towns…you know, taggers and such. The wrong element. And so, I've gotten everyone to chip in sixty dollars a month for a twenty-four hour security company. To patrol. It's been very effective. I'll stop by later on if you're interested and bring you the brochure. I've got lots of other people on file—

JACK

Good, 'cause the sooner I can get a list of anyone who doesn't clean up after their dogs, or…

GLORIA

(*Forced laugh.*) Well, not *those* people. You're a kick. More like plumbers, electricians, tree trimmers—

JACK

Bail bondsmen—

BEN

(*Overriding.*) That would be great.

GLORIA

Yes, because we never know when we might need a referral, right?

JACK

Can I call you "Mommy"?

BEN

Jack!

JACK

I'm *kidding!* She knows I'm kidding… (*To her.*) …right?

GLORIA

Oh, I do. Kidding is a textbook example of covering one's pain. (*To Jack, with great empathy.*) I'm so sorry for your loss. Every boy needs a good dad. Anyway, I best be getting back. (*Turning.*) Great wall for a flatscreen.

BEN

We don't really watch…could I give you a tour of the…?

(*Jack glares.*)

GLORIA

(*Backing out.*) No, no. I just dropped by to…you know.

JACK

(*Aside.*) Snoop.

BEN

Nothing's hooked up yet, so we can't even offer a— How about some champagne?

(*Jack kicks him.*)

Ow!

(*Gloria passes up through the arch, Ben following.*)

GLORIA

Oh, don't trouble yourselves. I'm in a big rush today. (*Sing-song.*)

Both kids at practice, tennis lesson. Ta-ta 'til soon! (*She's out, sound of front door closing behind her.*)

JACK

(*Ferocious whisper.*) Are you fucking kidding me?

BEN

You kicked me!

JACK

You offered her the Cristal?!

(*Sound of door reopening.*)

BEN

Shh!

(*Gloria crosses to right arch, takes a breath and speaks with determination.*)

GLORIA

I'm sorry. I do just want to say one more thing…I hope you boys won't be too loud.

JACK

(*Bridling.*) How do you mean?

GLORIA

In every way. We have children here. It's a family street.

(*Stunned, Jack and Ben look at each other.*)

I know you'll understand.

(*Gloria resumes her exit, Ben escorting.*)

Anyway, think about the security fee and good luck with the move-in. Bye-bye!

(*The front door closes again. Ben re-enters.*)

BEN

So much for the welcoming committee. God, you were rude.

JACK

Me? Her breath was like an open grave. What was her name?
Charmer?

BEN

Chalmers. (*Goes to stage right window.*) How long you think before
the whole block knows?

JACK

By sundown.

BEN

She's not even the Evangelical.

JACK

Christ, you mean there's worse?

BEN

(*Shaking head no.*) She's from *across* the street. Evangelicals, that
way.

JACK

And to think I waved to her when I pulled up. "Boys"?

(*Front bell, Ben goes to get it.*)

Christ, she's back. Don't answer it—Ben!

BEN (off)

Jumpin' Jehoshaphat, that's a huge spray! Do I need to sign?

(*Beat, Jack runs to stage right window to see.*)

Thanks, guy.

(*Door closes. Ben reenters with a large spray of flowers.*)

(*Reading card.*) It's from Ralph and the gang at your office.

(*Jack looks for and finds a corner for the bouquet right.*)

JACK

Now *that's* a proper house warmer. Throw those bear claws out.

BEN

Fat chance. (*Change of subject.*) Hey, what about these floors, huh?

JACK

(*Listless.*) You worked fast. The ink on the deed is barely dry—

BEN

Wait 'til you see what I did in the yard.

JACK

I could see from the driveway. The portico's amazing without Boston Ivy.

BEN

A little rotted. Good thing the Fenwicks had it tented. I found termite damage. I guess we're going to have to keep an eye on that. C'mere, look at this lawn slope…

(*He guides Jack to stage left door.*)

Think "infinity pool." Think wisteria-covered pergola. We could eat out there summers. Maybe all year with a propane heater. Or one of those open pit fireplace things…a chiminea!

JACK

We won't need one with all the burning crosses.

BEN

Hey, look…look at this— (*He crosses up to paint samples on wall.*) I picked up some great paint chips this morning. (*Holds a yellow one up to a purple splotch.*) Aren't they wild? Look…

JACK

Ah, Lakers. (*Beat.*) I like that one.

BEN

I know, right? Now think of it next to this… (*Holding them side by side.*) Right? For the trim, maybe? In one room? Or…you know what I think would be really amazing? All the other colors we've picked are so cool and muted…I think we should make at least one room pop! A total circus fantasy. I mean, like these colors, but with polka-dots and moonbeams.

JACK

(*Giggling.*) Polka-dots?

BEN

Why not? We totally let it rip, just in one room. Like Warhol's Factory.

JACK

Not in the kitchen.

BEN

No.

JACK

And not the master bedroom either. I'd wake up hankering for heroin.

BEN

I was thinking the nursery…

(*Jack tenses up. Long pause.*)

JACK

What's that mean, Ben?

BEN

Why not? In maybe a year or two? Once we're settled. It could be so much fun.

JACK

(*Beat. Staring at him.*) We've never been able to agree on kids.

BEN

That was then. We could. What are we setting all this up for? I mean, with the friends we have and our pooled resources…it's just kind of a perfect next step. Otherwise it's all about…accumulating *things*.

JACK

My mother will swoop down.

BEN

I love her, but she can't stay longer than a month.

JACK

A month?! God forbid. An afternoon. (*Beat.*) Are we talking adopting?

BEN

(*Encouraged.*) Or?

JACK

Or turkey basters?

BEN

There's all different…engineering possibilities. Every house needs a kid.

JACK

This one's had its share. (*Unconvinced. Beat.*) I'll have to think about it.

BEN

Of course. And…you know…we'll talk more…about it?

JACK

A lot.

BEN

Sure.

> (*Unable to control himself, he attempts a big hug, but Jack resists.*)

JACK

But not all the time, because you know what happens when couples get too focused on kids or pets. They lose sight of each other, like

Sean and Vinnie.

BEN

(*Putting arms around him.*) I don't think that's going to happen to us. Oh, hold on a sec. I found something in the yard today I want to show you.

> (*Ben rushes off left, leaving a dazed Jack for a few beats.*
> *Then…a sound—a cat, or a baby?—emanating from behind*
> *the basement door. A frisson shudders through Jack. He*
> *crosses to the door, listens…*)

JACK

(*To basement door.*) Benny? (*Beat.*) Did you go down the…?

> (*A sudden, distinct baby's wail coming from within. Jack*
> *jumps back in fright and crouches nervously on the staircase*
> *as Ben re-enters holding a small broken piece of concrete*
> *that has Jack's parents' initials carved in a heart.*)

BEN

Look what I unearthed under the lemon tree—! (*Sees Jack's condition.*) Jack, what's the matter?

JACK

(*Pale, he starts to get up but is very dizzy. Ben helps.*) I, uh…I'm not…

BEN

You're scaring me.

JACK

(*Feigning composure. Of Ben's find.*) Oh, look at that. That's my parents' initials. (*Woozy again.*) Ben, do me a favor and check that basement door.

> (*Bewildered, Ben does. Opens it, looks down, closes it.*)

You see anything? A cat?

BEN

Cat? Jack…what…what did *you* see?

JACK

It's all this "kid" talk, I think. (*Beat.*) Ben?

BEN

Did you eat anything today?

JACK

No…coffee.

BEN

I think you're having some sort of episode. Stay, I'll get you a bear claw.

> (*Ben exits left to kitchen. Jack's dazed. Ben returns with bear claw.*)

JACK

(*A bite.*) Thanks. (*Chews a beat, smiles.*) You think I'm freaking out?

BEN

A little. Is it the talk about the kid, the house, or just low blood sugar?

JACK

(*With mouth full.*) Thirty-three and a third percent of each. (*Of the food.*) Damnit, this is good.

BEN

Yeah. They always are, damnit. (*Beat.*) You know, as far as the kid goes it just feels like the right time now. Home-wise. Hormone-wise.

JACK

(*Chewing and musing.*) Your father's an alcoholic.

BEN

Yeah? As well as a minister. Your father dropped dead of a heart attack at forty-three. And your point would be?

JACK

Just sayin'…we should tread carefully around the gene pools before we take the plunge, right?

BEN

(*Facetiously.*) You know, you're onto something. (*Moving in threateningly.*) Let me take a closer look at those back molars?

JACK

Stop it.

BEN

There's a lot of baldness on your mother's side, isn't there? And you're not very good with hand tools…shit, I gotta rethink this whole thing.

JACK

Stop it. You're like Josef Mengele.

BEN

Thank you, counselor. Court adjourned while the jury deliberates on DNA.

JACK

(*Thoughtfully.*) Actually, with all the lezzies we know…Sue and Karen, Midge and Lambshanks… (*He shrugs.*) They're always talking about turkey basters and dixie cups. I gotta think…truth is, there are a lot of kids that are just *out there* already…the not-wanted babies.

BEN

Special-needs kids.

JACK

Risky, but…maybe worth it. If you believe what you hear on *This American Life*.

(*Ben kisses him, Jack submits.*)

Mmm… (*Pulls away.*) Hey, don't think you can sell me on this by getting into my pants.

(*Another kiss.*)

Well, maybe a little…

(*Again, and Jack pulls away, feeling fully himself again.*)

Before you go any further I have to tell you something.

BEN

You're pregnant?!

JACK

(*Shakes his head no. Beat.*) I'm not gay.

BEN

Oh, good. Then we can sleep together without feeling guilty.

JACK

And Gloria can bring us bear claws…

JACK & BEN

…in bed!

(*Ben dances around, lighthearted.*)

BEN

Look at us, Jack! We're here. We got it! Your parents' old house!
Damn! Who'da thunk it, huh? The two of us in suburbia?

JACK

(*Wincing.*) We should have bought that place in Key West.

BEN

And do what, snorkel? You can't swim.

JACK

West Hollywood then. That house was a Schindler.

BEN

And it was repped by a swindler. Those are ghettos.

JACK

Yes! *Ghettos. That's* what I'm talking about. *Living among our kind,* and Black people, Hassids, Central Americans! A melange of all the above with a nice little bodega on the corner where some sweet Haitian mammy makes a great goat stew. "High five, Leroy!" "Good shabbos to you, Rabbi!"

                              BEN

C'mon Jack…you were born here. So, it's a little white bread…

                              JACK

A little? It's as white as you can get without laundry bleach.

                              BEN

(*Losing ground.*) Yeah, well…it's convenient.

                              JACK

To what? Conversion therapy? They're already asking me to butch down and I haven't even planted a begonia. Note to self: You've always hated suburbs.

                              BEN

Hey, it's a house of our own. A craftsman. We got what we wanted.

                              JACK

(*Beat.*) Our "forever house." (*Sourly.*) And for just sixty dollars more a month we can protect ourselves from all the other outcasts encroaching on Earthly Delights—simply Google "gloria.com."

                              BEN

Now listen, your Ben ain't gonna let anyone… (*Nod in Gloria's direction.*) …besmirch his fella's happiness today. (*Beating chest, Tarzan-style.*)

JACK

"Besmirch." Good one. While we be smoochin', they besmirch. (*Off Ben's disapproval.*) What? I'm conjugating.

BEN

No you're not. You're caving in to paranoia. I know that look on your face.

JACK

What look?

BEN

That "Don't mind me, I'm just an undeserving middle school outcast!" look. (*Beat.*) Oh, I get what's happening here. *Caveat emptor*, right?

JACK

That would be "buyer *beware*." After the fact, it's complete and unqualified *remorse.*

BEN

(*Locking eyes.*) Stop it. We made this commitment, we agreed. This is day one. You're not being bullied, bashed, or harassed anymore. We're respectable now. Free to marry in fifty states. We've assimilated.

(*Jack objecting.*)

We *have.* We have good jobs. I'm a teacher for crissakes. And you...Mr. Newly Appointed Executive V.P. at Hi-TechTonics, Inc...

JACK

(*Warming, quotes Gilbert & Sullivan's* Pirates of Penzance.) "I am the very model of a modern major general…"

BEN

We'll pass muster. We'll mind our own business, put in a drought-tolerant front yard, re-shingle and…before you know it they'll be sending their husbands around under the pretext of borrowing my Allen wrenches…

JACK

(*Relenting.*) …and just three hours later we'll be walking them through Ben and Jack's handy tips on home improvement.

BEN

Exactly.

JACK

"*Never* mix ammonia with bleach…" I'll wear something slinky…

BEN

Hey.

JACK

(*Back at it.*) Why the hell do we have to be properly groomed and dedicated to raising property values before we're considered acceptable?

BEN

Because we suck dick, Jack.

JACK

I told you I'm not—//

BEN

(*Overlapping.*) —"gay," I heard you. But you sure are "talented."

JACK

(*Coyly.*) You mean it?

BEN

Come on upstairs.

> (*Ben grabs the champagne, takes Jack's hand and begins to lead him toward the upstage staircase. As they climb, Jack grabs the Bed Bath & Beyond bag with his free hand.*)

A brand new TempurPedic awaits your first impression.

JACK

(*Mimicking Gloria's voice.*) "We have children here!"

BEN

Shut up.

JACK

(*Playfully covering his posterior with bag.*) Will it hurt?

BEN

Shut up.

> (*They exit upstairs. From off, we hear their laughter, a pop of a champagne cork, deep moans. Suddenly, from behind the basement door, a distinct wail of a baby. Beat/silence above, then more wails.*)

257

BEN (off)

What's the matter?

JACK (off)

Ben, shh…

(*Another round of wails.*)

(*In hushed tones.*) Did you hear that?

BEN (off)

It's the water heater—

JACK (off)

No, Ben, shh. I think there's a cat. Or Gloria's back. Get off me, go look.

(*Ben appears shirtless at the top of the stairs.*)

Well? She there?

BEN

Hello? (*He looks over the banister.*) I hear no evil, I see no evil… I'm coming back to bed. (*He exits off up left.*)

JACK (off)

What are you talking abou—

(*He appears, disheveled, his shirt undone.*)

You hear that? It's in the basement. I'm gonna go down and look. (*Jack picks up the initialed rock and proceeds down.*)

BEN (off)

(*Of Jack holding rock.*) What are you gonna do with that, kill spiders? Come to bed!

(*Stealthily, Jack proceeds down.*)

I was in the basement half the morning. I'm telling you, you're hearing pipes. It's old plumbing. Son of a— Where the fuck is my shirt?

(*Jack approaches the basement door. The laughter begins again, a last barrage. Jack puts his fist on the doorknob, silently mouths…*)

JACK

ONE…TWO….THREE…

(*He swings open the door and steps onto the landing. He sees something terrifying below, jolts back.*)

AHHHHH!!!!!!!!!!!!!!!

(*Ben runs onto the upper landing.*)

BEN

JACK!

(*Jack blacks out, sliding to the floor. Blackout.*)

<u>Scene 2</u>

(A police red-top is flashing off right. Several hours later…dusk. Lights fade up on Jack down center staring upstage at the basement door. Upstage of the arch, we can hear Ben bidding farewell to policemen.)

BEN (off)

Thanks, Officer! We really appreciate it! Don't forget to let us know if anything turns up. Watch that mailbox post! There ya go. Bye-bye now!

(We hear the front door close—red-top fades—and Ben enters the room, leans against the archway, staring at Jack.)

JACK

Ben, am I going insane? There was a little kid in the basement, laughing at me. Could this be early onset schizophrenia?

BEN

Too late, you're in your thirties. Look, the cops scoured the house *and* the neighborhood, door to door. They're on it. We filed a report. I don't know what else we can do short of tearing up the floorboards.

JACK

Tear up the floorboards.

BEN

Babe, you really think that's the best way to introduce ourselves to the neighborhood our very first day here? First cop cars in the driveway, then some late-night demolition?

(*Jack crosses to the cellar door, puts his ear against it.*)

BEN

(*At Jack's action.*) What are you listening for?

(*Jack doesn't answer, just crosses down, checks windows. Ben heads to the kitchen, speaks from off.*)

You hungry?

(*Beat. Ben reenters, an open carton of Talenti and two spoons, sees Jack.*)

I checked twice, the cops checked. Drop it! Nobody's here but us.

(*Jack persists.*)

Hey, Sherlock! I asked if you're hungry?

(*No reply. Ben eats a spoonful.*)

I picked up some Talenti this afternoon.

(*Jack scowls.*)

Jack, you passed out. Eat. Look, I got dairy-free chocolate coconut.

(*He starts to eat more, feels Jack's eyes on him*).

What?

JACK

It's comforting to know that in a crisis your idea of consolation is caloric.

BEN

It's one way to lure the kid out... (*Under breath.*) ...*if* there was one—

JACK

If? I saw…forget it. (*Beat.*)

BEN

Eat! (*Proffers spoonful.*) Okay, abstain. (*He eats.*) We should call the realtor.

JACK

I told you the moment I set eyes on him I didn't trust him. He's smarmy.

BEN

He might know…*something.* (*Offhandedly.*) Maybe the place is haunted. (*Off Jack's look.*) Just call him. But be civil, okay? Don't verbally assault the guy like you're prone to—and—//

JACK

What are you talking about? I'm diplomacy personified. (*Of the Talenti.*) You're gonna get it all over.

BEN

Jack! None of this is making our first day in the house easier!

JACK

Hey, come with me. I'll stage a little re-enactment of what I saw… (*Jack heads to cellar door.*) …and you'll see for yourself who's daft and who's…

(*His voice trailing off. Ben follows, remaining in view as Jack disappears down, bellowing from offstage…*)

Hello-oo? You down there, little guy…? We got Talenti here, hello?

> (*Jokingly, Ben slams the basement door shut, frightening Jack out of his wits. Jack, panicked, tries the locked door 'til Ben opens it.*)

BEN!

> (*Ben is laughing as Jack re-emerges.*)

That's not funny, Ben! The door locks from the outside. We've got to find that *kid* and *take* him down to the police station before they're back here with a warrant—//

BEN

Jack, show me "that kid." Where's he hiding? Besides Gloria and the cops, I haven't even seen one trace of anyone but you. You say *you* have, but—

JACK

Do you really think I'm making this up?

BEN

I didn't say that.

JACK

But you're thinking it.

BEN

I'm thinking if there was a kid here he must have…slipped out or off or—

JACK

Oh, don't give me that. With all the child abductions going on across

America? This is exactly how innocent people can get incriminated—Jesus, we've already got the snoops out in force…you got Talenti all down the front of your shirt. (*Crossing off left.*) Come into the kitchen.

BEN

(*Follows him off.*) What do you suggest we do?

JACK (off)

(*Losing it.*) I don't know! What would Tony Soprano do?!

> (*They exit. From off right, we hear the sound of knocks on the front door.* BILL DIMMELWICH, *a sixty-something realtor with an edge of dissipation and a smarmy, obsequious smile, pokes his head into the room from stage right. His tie's askew; he's a little tipsy.*)

BILL

Yoo-hoo! Knock-knock. Anybody home?

> (*Silence from off. Bill steps fully into the upstage arch, a cellphone at the ready in one hand, briefcase in the other.*)

Shit. They got rid of that shag already… (*Under breath.*) No shags for fags. I liked that shag. (*Calling out.*) Hello-ooo!

> (*Ben and Jack fly back on and skid to a halt when they see who it is.*)

Hello, boys. Sorry to just barge in. I knocked, but nobody answered.

JACK

Oh, hi Bill. (*Covering.*) We were…just about to call you.

BILL

Gloria Chalmers reached me out of concern. She said there was some police activity so I—//

BEN

Oh, yeah. It was nothing really. We—//

JACK

(*Correcting Ben.*) No, actually, it was *something.* I called them because—//

BEN

Something scared Jack down in the basement. Just, you know…first-day jitters.//

BILL

Oh, I've been there! A little buyer's remorse can wreak havoc. That's one good reason why I always come prepared: (*Reveals flask.*) Bill's very own First Day First-Aid Kit!

(*Offers. They decline.*)

Here's to no regrets. (*He chug-a-lugs.*)

BEN

Yeah, he actually thought he heard a…prowler or something. Gloria had warned us about a certain, y'know, *element* sneaking around, and—//

BILL

Oh, pay no attention to Glo—//

JACK

You just did.

BEN

I'm just gonna do one more pass around the perimeters. 'Scuse me…

(*He heads down the basement. Another awkward pause.*)

BILL

(*To Jack.*) You fellas sure don't hesitate to make a place your own, do you?

JACK

(*Snide.*) Oh, yeah. We're determined to put the homo back in homeowner.

BILL

(*Taken aback.*) Do I detect a bit of self-loathing, Jack? (*Gesturing at floors.*) All I'm saying, I'm impressed.

JACK

(*Contrite.*) You mean the floors? Yeah, well, Ben…we're just trying to work out a few options for what we should—//

BILL

(*A dog with a bone.*) Beautiful hardwood, just as I predicted. Earthly Delights was famous for quality materials.

(*Beat, Jack pacing.*)

I happened to be closing on another house nearby when I got Gloria's call so I thought I'd drop by. It's coming along. That portico—

(*Jack's going nuts. Bill can't help but notice. Bill taps*

briefcase.)

Hey, look...I brought some "spirit stuff," y'know, just in case. Holy water, Native American rattle and sage—//

JACK

(*This gets his attention.*) Sage?

BEN

(*Emerging from basement.*) No sign of any intruders down there. No siree. Coast is clear.

JACK

(*Between his teeth.*) Where were you expecting the kid to be? Behind the water heater?

BEN

The water heater's two inches from the wall, but sure, okay... (*He heads upstage to check the basement, calling as he goes.*) HEY, LITTLE KID? YOU SQUEEZED FLAT BACK THERE?

BILL

Kid? What kid?

BEN

(*Re-enters.*) Nope. (*Heading upstairs, eager to avoid Bill.*) 'Scuse me while I check *upstairs*! (*He bounds up and off.*)

BILL

You guys have a kid?

JACK

We don't. I do. In the playpen of my mind.

BILL

Hey, you fellas oughta have a kid. You really oughta.

JACK

We'll take it under advisement.

BILL

Well, why not? They're a constant source of distraction. My kid used to hide behind the trash compactor sometimes. (*Laugh.*) To this day I can't figure out how he fit. He'd emerge for suppertime all sweaty and scorched… (*Off Jack's look.*) He's close to forty now. Doesn't talk to dear old dad anymore. Fuck him, as they say. (*Another swig.*)

JACK

Look, there *was* a kid. Not ours. He must have been…*left* here, or…yes, because I remember seeing him on the first walk-through…I think it was *that* kid. Not *him*-him, his *photograph*…I *remember*…when you showed us the house, that first day…maybe it was, what's her name? Doreen's kid…he's…short, right? Doreen Fenwick's kid? Like two years old? Real pale… (*Petering out.*) The whole family was short, no? Maybe he ran away? Because of the shortness thing?

(*Awkward pause. Bill takes out his car key ring.*)

Lexus, huh? You lease or—?

(*Bill looks at him sourly.*)

Oh, come on, look…*somebody's* kid was hiding in the basement this afternoon! Can't you just call the Fenwicks? See if they're missing someone?

BILL

I seriously don't think…okay, look, if it'll ease your mind I'll text Doreen. (*Of his new phone.*) Bear with me, I'm still learning how to work these fucking contraptions… (*He plays with his phone as the doorbell rings.*)

JACK

(*To Ben, who bounds downstairs.*) Who could that be…child services?

> (*Ben steps off right in the direction of front door. We hear it open.*)

BEN

Oh, hi.

GLORIA

(*Entering.*) Everything okay? I was driving back from the club a few minutes ago and saw the police…

BEN

Everything's fine.

BILL

Jack thought he saw a kid in the basement.

GLORIA

A *kid?!*

BEN

(*Pulling Jack up left for a private confab.*) Behave…//

GLORIA

(*A diversionary tactic.*) Bill! You scalliwag, what are you up to? No sooner had I called you when lo and behold, Ed said "Isn't that Bill Dimmelwich's hybrid SUV?"

(*A cacophany ensues.*)

BILL	JACK
Hello, Gloria! Deirdre's at the club.//	(*To Ben, fierce.*) You didn't have to stage an elaborate charade. Why did you do that?//
GLORIA	
I know *where* she is, dimwit! I just came back from our tennis lesson. You better watch out, Mister…that Serbian coach is the dreamiest thing since George Clooney. She tell you about him? (*"J" as "y".*) Jan?	**BEN**
	(*Aside.*) No kid, Jack. There is no kid. Not a trace anywhere…//
	JACK
	You think I'm nuts, don't you?
BILL	**BEN**
Oh, yes…I know all about *Jan*.	I don't, but…relax, will ya?

BILL

(*Suddenly wriggling.*) Ooh, that tickles…what's vibrating? (*He feels in pocket.*) Ha! I'm getting a text. (*Takes out phone, reads it.*) It's Doreen in Arizona.

JACK

Now at least maybe we'll find out something concrete—//

(*Bill stops him in his tracks.*)

BILL

Hold on, Jack, hold on—she writes... (*Reading.*) "Kids in back seat, on way back from recital, hyphen. Ginny won first prize, exclamation point. Loving Scottsdale, smiley face. Will call 2nite, period." (*Askance.*) So it looks like she's got both her kids with her after all...

JACK

(*Turning, catches sight.*) Ben, is that someone out in the yard? (*Exits down left.*)

BEN

'Scuse me a sec. (*Exits after Jack.*) JACK!

GLORIA

What's that all about?

BILL

(*Of Jack.*) The sidekick's a bit neurotic.

GLORIA

(*In confidence.*) I'm a smidge miffed at you, Dimmelwich.

BILL

I know, Glo, I know, but I had to take their offer. The property was on the market two years! (*Sotto voce.*) Give me some credit.

(*He takes a few steps away from her to swallow a short pull from a concealed flask. She follows, not noticing.*)

GLORIA

Bill, this is Herringbone Way! (*Sotto voce.*) As soon as I found out about the short sale, and that you would be handling it, I faxed you two lists of interested parties, Bill. "Clean" people. The *crème de la crème*. Not…Siegfried & Roy. You couldn't have done better than sell it to people of faith, like Reverend Monahan, his lovely wife, Mona, their beautiful towhead children. Patsy Pillsbury? These people have impeccable credentials. We could have had upright citizens moving in today—donors to the church, the Family Research Council, Ted Cruz's campaign! Somehow you just ignored all that so that… (*She looks off left.*) I don't know why. And now the Lady Gaga Brigade has landed to plant their rainbow flag. Oh, stick around, Mister, if you want to see some real abnormal behavior. These are the very people who throw nude pool parties, in the *afternoon!* Who blast their Donna Summer collections all hours, every season…who believe that "freedom's just another word for nothing left to lose." My God…they will flaunt their agenda in the worst possible way, Bill.

     (*Jack enters unseen, listens.*)

"Marriage equality"? Please! I hope you checked to see they're not registered sex offenders.

BILL

Oh, Gloria, please.

GLORIA

And what's this kid-in-the-basement thing really about?

BILL

I don't know. (*Another swig.*)

GLORIA

(*A jolt.*) Doreen always said there was something creepy about this place...did you sell a *stigmatized* property, Dimmelwich?!

(*He scoffs.*)

Don't scoff! I'm the one who'll have to draw my drapes every day, not you. I'm the one who'll have to squint my eyes dashing between the front door and the car, to blot out the, the...

(*Jack's in. Gloria about-faces.*)

Hi, there! I was just telling Bill how excited I am to see what happens to our property values now that people with a little decorative "bonhomie" have arrived to spruce up the block.

JACK

Really?

GLORIA

(*Affecting patois.*) Sho' nuff.

JACK

(*Sniffs air.*) Because there's an acrid smell of vitriol in the air...

GLORIA

Bill, dear...? Back me up here.

BILL

(*Busy with phone, dissembling.*) Goddamn, it's Planet of the Apps!

JACK

(*Quoting.*) Article 12, Universal Declaration of Human Rights, Eleanor Roosevelt: "No one shall be subjected to arbitrary interference with his privacy, family, home, nor to attacks upon his honor or reputation…" (*He sings "America the Beautiful" continuously, blocking her way.*) "O Beautiful for spacious skies…"

GLORIA

(*Trying to cross to door.*) I best be getting back before I burn my brownies. Ta-ta!

(*Jack's blocking her exit, singing.*)

Pardon me, please. Young man…I said excuse me, please. (*Finally, roaring.*) BACK THE FUCK OFF!

(*Jack stops. Gloria pushes her way past him and out the door. Jack follows, resuming singing, then turning back as Ben returns, taking in the insanity.*)

JACK

"…above the fruited plain…"

BEN

Jack! What's going on?

JACK

(*Stops singing.*) Assimilated, huh?

(*As he leads Ben left to the kitchen, Bill whoops, crocked.*)

BILL

WOO-HOO! The sweet spot, YES!!! (*Heading left to garden door.*)

Where's that old lemon tree? (*Now he's singing, à la Trini Lopez.*)
"Lemon tree very pretty…" (*He exits.*)

JACK

What the hell? Ben, he's shitfaced. He's not staying here. Call an
Uber.//

BEN

We can't let him drive like that. (*Taking out phone.*) Let's get some
food in him. I'll go get Thai takeout?

BILL

(*Re-entering with lemons, progressively drunker.*) Fellas, fellas,
fellas…Thai takeout sounds like heaven… (*Hands them the lemons.*)
And as a token of my appreciation, put it on my credit card—

(*He slides it out. Ben hesitates.*)

Take it, it's legit. Check the expiration. Sky's the limit, don't scrimp.
Tonight, we celebrate! Let's pig OUT!

(*They look at each other but he's insistent.*)

Fellas, don't even think about resisting me. It's *on me*! Happy to do
it. Go! I'll stick around here, do the old once over… (*Does a little
soft shoe.*) …attic to cellar, curb to closets, 'til you come back with
the chow-chow. If there's any mischief afoot around here, yours truly
is the man who got you into it, so yours truly will sort it all out. Got
my sage, got some incantations…

(*He nearly falls, but Ben catches him.*)

Scout's honor. Love those scouts. All those khaki shorts and colorful ribbons. Cute as hell.

(*Jack crosses right to sit but Bill now pursues him.*)

Oh, and just to set the record straight… (*Confidentially.*) I'm bi myself. (*Beat.*) You know what I'm sayin' by "bi"? Bye-bye! No, I'm bi-*sexual.* Shh. Don't let Glo know. (*Wags his finger insistently.*) Not Ms. Snoop-Snoop. (*He staggers again, Ben catching.*)

BEN

That's…wow, just great. Really, I'm, uh, glad, and…kind of touched that you told us that, Bill. Wow. I wouldn't have ever…thanks for sharing.

BILL

Well, duh. Who better with? Right? I just want you to bear that in mind. No discrimination here. Not testing those waters currently. But I have, you know…dipped in that pool. (*He drops to his knees.*) Oh yeah. Loved me some man meat, yessiree. Slurp, slurp. Gobble, gobble. (*And he's on the floor.*) Shh. Just a few winks here…nighty night, now.

(*Ben is dumbstruck. Jack, is too.*)

BEN

Shit. (*Of Bill.*) Jack? What do we do?

JACK

(*Rising, heading upstairs.*) Get the Buddha's feast and chicken satay. I'll fluff a pillow for the boozer.

(*At a loss, Ben slips Bill's credit card in prone Bill's jacket*

276

pocket and heads out the front door, Jack calling after.)
And don't forget chopsticks! The forks don't get delivered 'til
tomorrow.

*(As we hear Ben's car start and pull away, Jack descends,
places a sheet over the prostrate Bill as ... lights fade.)*

Scene 3

*(**Strange Interlude**: An hour later. Dark. The living room is lit dimly by the spill of greenish exterior street lights—stage right window—and yellow yard light, stage left only. Bill's prone body is still visible on the floor, covered by a sheet. Jack and Ben are gone. A flash of heat lightning, then thunder.*

Sound of front door opening. Visible iPhone flashlight. Gloria slips in quietly, shines her phone light downstage to scan living room, missing Bill on the floor.)

GLORIA

Bill? I see your car's still here.

(He groans and she spots his body, leans close, lifts an edge of the sheet. In hushed tone, on her cell to her husband.)

Silly Billy. He's out cold. Can you text Dierdre, honey? I don't want a repeat of that fiasco at the country club… *(Snooping about.)* Of course, but I don't see them. Maybe they've had a change of heart— if only…don't worry, I'll be careful. I just want to see for myself if they've abducted some poor child. *(Signaling with phone light to husband from window.)* You know me and a good mystery…well, keep your eyes on the driveway. Bye.

(*She creeps up to the cellar door, slowly opens it and steps onto the landing looking down. Beat. Then a breeze and the door slams shut, locking her inside. LIGHTNING/THUNDER. She screams.*)

Bill sits up with an ugly grunt, the sheet over him. He hears the sound of Gloria behind the cellar door, trying the doorknob, whimpering. A shadow passing over his face.)

BILL

(*Sardonically.*) Alright. So there *is* a kid…hiding down there…
(*Listens at door.*) Fucking devil's spawn…

(*He moves to and opens his briefcase. Ritualistically, Bill begins to take implements of exorcism out and arrange them on the floor—a sage stick, a small plastic vial of holy water, a rattle. He calls out.*)

I'm gonna get you, little fucker.

(*LIGHTNING/THUNDER. From upstairs, a groggy Jack calls.*)

JACK (off)

Ben? Is that you?

(*Bill removes his jacket, rolls up his sleeves, picks up the sage, lights it, and the rattle, shaking it as he moves up to the cellar door. Gloria whimpers.*)

BILL

Come out, come out, wherever you are. (*He spritzes.*) I don't know if you're real or some fucking figment from hell, but you're too late to queer this deal, buddy. So let's just let the gay guys be. Whaddaya say? The check's in the bank already. The deed is signed. (*He blows smoke under door.*) You hear that, lil' buddy? Signed!

> (*Shaking the rattle around the perimeter of the door, then stopping to listen. Silence for a beat. LIGHTING/ THUNDER. Then…*)

> *Gloria's eerie shriek from within startles him and he jumps back. From upstairs, we hear…*)

JACK (off)

BEN?!

BILL

(*Yelling up.*) Ben's not back yet!

> (*The banging increases. Bill begins dancing hypnotically, stomping about, chanting gibberish. The light on the staircase comes on, saturating the area with color, and Jack appears on the landing in his underwear. Another shriek from the cellar.*)

YA YA YA YA, HIYA-KAHLA-HIYA-KAHLA, GET THE FUCK OUT OF HERE, GET THE FUCK OUT OF HERE! CRAVEN PARIAH! (*Another shriek.*) NO ONE QUEERS A DEAL ON

DIMMELWICH. I'M *LEGIT!* UNDERSTAND? I'M *LICENSED!*

JACK

Is he back? Did you see him, too? It's that same kid…catch him,

Bill—//

> (*Meantime, more thunder and the eerie sound of a child's*
> *laughter, building throughout.*)

BILL

YOU SATANIC PIECE OF SHIT. Y'HEAR ME? What are you,

some godforsaken *GANGBANGER?* Some phantom scum from

hell…?

> (*Bill crosses to and shakes open the sheet with one hand, puts*
> *the other on the doorknob…*)

YOU READY? YOU READY…?

> (*…and with a wild flourish swings open the cellar door,*
> *throwing the sheet over Gloria's head as she scrambles*
> *toward the front door.*)

GOTCHA!

> (*He struggles with her stage left.*)

GLORIA

(*Muffled cries.*) LET GO…LET GO OF ME! PLEASE, LET ME

GO!

JACK

What the hell is going on?

BILL

(*Struggling.*) I hooked your intruder—ugh—be still!

JACK

That's not any old intruder. That's Gloria.

> (*From beneath the sheet, Gloria kicks Bill's shin, freeing*
> *herself and heading to the front door just as Ben is coming*
> *through it with an order of Thai takeout and a six-pack of*
> *Singha.*)

BILL

OW! GODDAMN, THAT HURT!

> (*He lets go. She scrambles out the door, Bill in hot pursuit.*
> *The sound of child laughing slowly crossfades with exterior*
> *downpour.*)

BEN

(*To Jack.*) What the hell was Gloria doing here? (*He looks off right.*)
Holy shit, she cold-cocked him—NO! Watch out for that mailbox!
(*Puts food down, exits right.*)

JACK

(*Ascending stairs, resigned to mayhem.*) If he forgot the chopsticks,
I'll kill him.

> (*Blackout.*)

Scene 4

(Forty-five minutes later. Storm's passed. Ambulance light flashes off right. Ben's at the front door, seeing off paramedics, who are just leaving.)

BEN (off)

...we will. We'll make sure he stays down. Thanks, you guys. You're the best. Oh, and watch out for that mailbox post as you're pulling out, 'kay? Bye-bye now!

(Ben shuts the door and enters to the foot of the stairs. Beat. Jack stands conniving his next move, then crosses paths with Ben to look in the Thai food bag.)

(Picks up sheet, jolly.) An exciting first day, huh? Cops, paramedics. How the hell did Gloria get in? I guess that's my fault. I should learn to lock that door. *(Beat.)* I think I'm going to move that mailbox post tomorrow. It looked good in the *Restoration Hardware* catalogue, but it's not working here.

(Jack now grabs the sheet from him, folding and refolding it. Ben continues, sotto voce, of Bill upstairs.)

Good thing you had the beds delivered early. That's some gash on his head.

(Approaching Jack, who avoids contact.)

You mad at me?

(*No response. Jack obviously stewing.*)

Can you believe the swing on that dame? (*Moves closer.*) You okay? What gives?//

JACK

Peachy. Couldn't be better. Only thing that could enhance my mood right now is a cerebral hemorrhage.

BEN

You *are* mad at me.

JACK

You forgot the chopsticks. Leave it at that. (*Takes sheet off up left.*)

BEN

I thought I… (*Crossing down, sotto voce, Jack returns.*) So? What are we going to do about…? (*Nods upstairs.*) Let him sleep it off, I guess.

JACK

And then what? Run a hot bubble bath and scrub his back while I iron his pants and bake his favorite cassoulet?

BEN

You're so sarcastic.

JACK

Benny—Jesus!

BEN

What?

284

JACK

Wasn't it just yesterday we were skipping through Bed Bath & Beyond?

BEN

Tuesday, actually. (*Ever the optimist.*) And tonight we're here!

JACK

We! (*Jack frantically points upstairs.*)

BEN

Okay. So he's…he's our first guest.

JACK

Our drunken realtor?

BEN

He's not going to be here all night. Trust me. Another hour, we'll nudge him awake, spruce him up, and send him on his way.

JACK

I don't know. Honestly, do you think we're cut out for owning property? For me, the whole endeavor is already desecrated.

(*Ben moves blithely up right to six-pack, grabs one.*)

Why is it *I* feel like that and you're in pig heaven?

BEN

(*Opening beer.*) Not.

JACK

Yes, Ben. Good-Samaritan pig heaven. Need I remind you of the spat we had at our yard sale?

285

BEN

We didn't need any of that stuff…your old orange iMac? Those at-risk kids could use it.

JACK

They wore better shoes than me! "At risk." You also gave away brand new yoga mats, a sleeping bag we used *once*…

BEN

We needed the closet space. (*Sips a beer.*) That's warm. Besides, you don't like yoga, you despise camping…

JACK

On *glaciers!* I froze my ass off!

BEN

You're exaggerating. There was barely an inch of snow in Yellowstone.

JACK

And a moose!

    (*Ben takes six-pack, exits left to kitchen. In the seconds he's gone, Jack hears the sound of a baby crying again*

Fuck, there it is again. (*Calling off.*) Ben, what are you doing?

BEN (off)

I'm putting the rest of the six-pack in the fridge.

    (*He re-enters, holding the Thai takeout bag and arranges food cartons on the floor as Jack circulates through the room, testing windows, doors, mumbling to himself, taking a few*

286

steps up the stairs to listen, losing courage, coming back down.)

You've got to calm down, babe. You're gonna get shingles.

BEN	JACK
I got #37–green beans and the garlic with fried tofu. #73–pud see yew, with shrimp. #104–garlic string beans, Buddha's feast. Medium spicy. No appetizers?	Look who's calling the kettle black. Shingles… (*He continues checking each nook and cranny.*)

JACK

You didn't get chicken satay?!

BEN

Did they forget the…? Uh, hold it a sec… (*He digs deep.*) Ah! Surprise—chicken satay! #3, with extra peanut sauce. You want Thai iced tea?

(*Jack tentatively approaches the basement door.*)

JACK

I'll be up all night. Fuck it, yeah. (*Jack takes a step onto the basement landing.*)

BEN

(*Searching bag.*) Where is the iced tea? (*Crossing out.*) Did I leave it in the car?

(*As Ben heads off right to investigate, Jack opens the basement door, summons courage and walks onto the lower landing. Instantly, the sound of child's laughter. Jack quickly emerges, ashen, slamming the basement door shut and leaning against the wall, hyperventilating.*

Ben enters right with bag containing Thai iced tea and chopsticks.)

BEN

Yep, 'twas in the car. As were these handy thing-a-ma-jigs.

JACK

(*Blinking back from a bad dream.*) Where were you?

BEN

I left these in the car. (*Jaunty.*) Oh, guess who was having dinner at the Thai place? The Evangelicals from next door, Pete and Francine. (*Realizing.*) What's the matter?

JACK

(*Jack begins to laugh hysterically.*) Ha-ha-ha…oh, we gotta talk, Mister. We've really got to talk.

BEN

Fine, but can we nosh while we chat, 'cause I'm starved out of my… (*Off Jack's look.*) Alright, go.

JACK

(*Beat. Taking a stand.*) Okay, Ben…I'm going to give you a quick synopsis of the plot up to this point, because you're obviously in a different movie. He, Bill… (*Pointing at ceiling.*) …is upstairs, courtesy of the paramedics, blottoed. While you, Ben… (*Pointing.*)

…wander off into the night to schmooze with Christian lunatics at Thai Town—// (*Points down left.*)

BEN

They're not lunatics, they're actually kind of great—//

JACK

Fine, *I'm* the lunatic!

BEN

Jack—

JACK

(*Holding hand up.*) Courtesy please! So that leaves me… (*Jabbing his chest with his thumb.*) …to wander about this… (*Circles finger in the air.*) …CRAZY FUCKING ASYLUM WE NOW CALL HOME, ALONE—//

BEN

Calm down, Jack. You're too worked up—

JACK

Am I? Too worked up? I *saw* a kid, standing *down there, just now—that's twice in one day!* (*Pointing to cellar.*) REALLY! (*Beat.*) Please stop looking at me like I'm speaking in tongues. I SAW HIM, DAMNIT! I'm not making it up. (*Points downstage to audience.*) Ask them, probably out there right now peering at us with binoculars as we speak.

BEN

(*Taking hold of him in an embrace.*) Jack, I love you. And I believe you. That's what I'm gonna keep returning to, no matter what. Okay?

   (*Jack slips from his embrace.*)

Now let's relax, eat something and we can talk about what we know is real and true, here now, and what's just some free-range anxiety.

JACK

What's real and true…I wish I knew. I just get a vibe here…

BEN

Like of what, a recovered memory?

JACK

Something. I don't know. I was in utero when we moved here and when Dad dropped dead I was purportedly in a playpen oblivious to such tragedies. An attitude I wish I had maintained. End of story as I know it.

BEN

And the beginning of ours. (*Beat.*) Maybe…maybe…

JACK

(*Real distress.*) You think I need to go back on Zoloft?

BEN

(*Putting his arm around him.*) Jack, Jack…it's been a very stressful first day. We need to eat. And then maybe…meds. We both need meds.

   (*They share a smile. Ben leads Jack up to food.*)

It's gonna be okay. Really, it's all okay. We knew this was going to be a big adjustment. It's just going to take some time for us

290

to…adjust.

JACK

I didn't get that memo.

BEN

And you know, Jack, maybe that… (*He looks toward cellar.*)
…the—

JACK

Go ahead, say it: "Stephen King phantom child only I can see…"

BEN

Maybe that *kid* is showing up now for a reason.

(*Turning sweet piano jazz on iPod, then proffering food.*)
Here, have some garlic string beans…

(*Jack relents and is drawn to the stairs by food. They settle
there to sup.*)

JACK

(*Mulling.*) "Showing up now…" So weird. (*Beat.*) I never told you
but…when I was hitting puberty, I used to have recurring dreams
about giving birth. They were always malevolent little monsters.
Friendly at first, but the moment I'd try to engage with one it would
go ballistic and tear my arm off.

(*They're both eating ravenously now.*)
Hmm. (*Beat.*) Long time since I thought of that.

BEN

Why have you never told me?

JACK

At what point in a relationship is it most conducive to reveal one's personal psychosis?

(*Ben shrugs.*)

Once—this was the freakiest dream—I was lying underwater in a pool looking up at the clear blue sky above—very peaceful—when into my view floats a school of embryos, right out of *2001*, only like a dozen of them, those big eyes staring down at me, blocking the light…

BEN

Shit.

JACK

Right? And if that isn't creepy enough, all at once, they open their mouths and let out a scream—one long, sustained note… (*He mimics it.*) …*ahh!* I woke the fuck up out of that one.

(*Beat. They chew in silence.*)

This is delicious. (*Lightening up, nonchalant.*) Okay, so maybe there's a ghost here. So? We'll handle it, right? We're manly men. We'll…perform an exorcism.

BEN

(*Reciting, quiet and trance-like.*) "That's what happens when ghosts get into the house. They try to frighten you with their beckoning fingers and clanking chains, not knowing that…that…" (*Beat.*) Ah! Can't remember the rest.

JACK

What the fuck is that?

BEN

Noël Coward, "Design for Living." I played Otto my sophomore year at Skidmore. Funny, that just popped into my head. (*On a drama club roll.*) "He thrusts his fists against the post and still insists he sees the ghost."

JACK

Will you stop?

BEN

Sorry. (*Beat.*) You haven't had one of those "malevolent kid" dreams since we're together, have you?

(*Jack mechanically shakes his head no.*)

So…maybe the damage is already healed.

JACK

Damage? (*Dubious.*) You mean like maybe the universe is telling us something?

BEN

It told me to go back to the bar when you didn't show up our first date.

JACK

That was a Craigslist mistake.

BEN

Just sayin'. It told us about this property…

JACK

"It"? What it? Don't get all Marianne Williamson on me. Before we got Bill-the-Bi-Realtor involved we found this listing on Craigslist.

BEN

(*Dawning.*) Jack, maybe Craigslist IS the universe.

JACK

We should check there for babies.

> (*Pause as each considers, then laughter.*)

BEN

I love you.

> (*He picks up food things, starts clearing them to the kitchen.*)

Let's go up. Try out that new mattress.

JACK

(*Of Bill.*) What about…?

BEN

He won't hear a thing. And even if he does, he's bi, remember?

JACK

Bi-polar.

> (*Ben returns, shuts off music, lights.*)

No, Ben… I don't have my lens cleaner, my Sonic-Care, my dental floss…

BEN

Skip them tonight. (*He reaches for Jack's hand.*)

JACK

I just had garlic string beans!

BEN

So did I.

> (*Ben exhales like a dragon, Jack feigns fainting. Ben pulls him up to the upper landing, but Jack halts to ruminate.*)

JACK

What a day, Benny.

BEN

Yeah. (*He takes one last look around.*) It's all ours now. Welcome home.

> (*Ben exits up but Jack lingers, sipping iced tea and prattling.*)

JACK

I think in a way the best place for a nursery would be in the basement. If I can just get over my…and I will! Especially if we get live-in help and subdivide it down there. Plus I'd be less embarrassed about painting polka dots and moonbeams on a basement wall, although I still think my mother will want to move in. The moment she hears we're…we're…what do you call it when gay people are pregnant? "Expecting" doesn't feel right… Anticipating? Adjudicating? Obfuscating?

BEN (off)

You've had too much Thai iced tea.

JACK

(*To self.*) Of course, we'll have to revisit the marriage question.

> (*Just as Jack begins to ascend, sound of baby's cry returns,
> underscored by Bach's Mass in B Minor "Agnus Dei." Jack
> quickly reappears, looking down into the living room with
> serious misgivings, and begins descending the stairs.*)

BEN (off)

Come to bed!

> (*Ignoring him, Jack crosses down to the basement door,
> slowly swings it open, an eerie light emanating. And into that
> light, Jack moves trance-like to stand at the top of the
> basement landing in profile, bravely looking down. The light
> grows in intensity from below, as the high pitched scream
> Jack described earlier coming from his "school of embryos"
> dream swallows all sound. But Jack makes a strong decision:
> He steps out of the basement entrance, slams the door shut,
> cutting off the sounds, and leans back in silence against the
> wall.*)

JACK

(*A prayer now.*) "There's no place like home." Please, Dorothy, let it be true.

BEN (off)

Come to bed!

JACK

(*After an intense moment, he comes back to his senses.*) Coming.

(And with that, he heads toward the staircase, to Ben, and bed as...lights fade.)

END OF ACT I.

ACT II

Scene 1

(*A year later. Lights up on basement nursery. Polka dots and moonbeams on the walls, but so gorgeously rendered that it works. The layout is almost an exact replica of the first act room above, with staircase upstage under which is a broom closet door, and a doorway down left to an offstage bath and laundry room, Humpty Dumpty painted on the door. Downstage the room is as empty as the Act I room was above save for a small stepladder upon which sits a boom box playing Prokofiev's "Peter and the Wolf." In one corner right are a few boxes containing an unassembled crib and assorted baby furniture. The windows stage right are high-set basement windows, through which morning light pours. The down left wall is windowless. After a few beats, we hear voices above: Jack and his mother Evelyn. She's loud.*)

EVELYN (off)

Oh, my God! You filled the whole place with stuff. Too much stuff! This is *not* how I remember it. You're homosexuals. You're supposed to like "spare" and have an appreciation for simplicity and clean lines. Like the Japanese. It's starting to look like your grandmother's house up here. I mean, you got nice things, but…

298

(Evelyn appears at the top of the stairs, followed by her son.)

JACK

(Moving past her quickly down the stairs.) Where's Ben? He was going to assemble that crib already… *(Stepping off left.)* Benny! You in the bathroom?

> *(Evelyn is frozen in her tracks on the stairs. Jack thinks she can barely contain her revulsion at the paint job, but her eye is on the crib box.)*

EVELYN

Jacky…

> *(He re-enters, sees her unease, and crosses to shut off the boom box.)*

JACK

(Beat.) I like it.

EVELYN

The paint job? It's very Cirque du Soleil. *(Holding up a hand.)* I know you're aiming for "Playland" but this way it's a little too—//

JACK

"Gayland?"

> *(She's silent.)*

Yeah, well, the idea is "cheerful."

> *(Evelyn sighs. She takes the last tentative steps down off the steps as if she might set off a landmine.)*

EVELYN

Your father came from cheerful. I never trust it. (*She shrugs.*) The
Irish. (*New tack.*) Can you tell me why the hell you're putting the
nursery in the basement? You make no sense. How you gonna hear
the baby cry?

JACK

EXACTLY! (*She frowns.*) Relax. We're interviewing live-in nannies
next week. Oh and Ma, FYI about fifty years ago some genius
invented the baby monitor—

EVELYN

I don't trust gizmos. My sister Sheila spent a fortune on alarms and
surveillance gadgets and still they kidnapped your cousin.

JACK

I didn't know Walter got kidnapped.

EVELYN

Before you were born. Why do you think they sent him off to
technical school? That ransom cost his entire college fund. Plus he
had that misshapen head.

(*A shared laugh.*)

JACK

Fascinating. Come look at the new bathroom. (*He crosses left.*)

EVELYN

(*As she follows.*) I hope it's properly ventilated. If not you'll get
mold. I had mold in Sunrise. Between that, the Gulf mishigas, the

mosquitoes…

(Jack's standing left with the bathroom door open, waiting for her reaction. She looks, appraising the new bathroom.)

JACK

What do you think?

EVELYN

(Beat, unimpressed.) New.

JACK

Ben did it. He always wanted the bathroom from *Psycho*. You like?

EVELYN

It's a bathroom. I've seen bathrooms. As bathrooms go, it's new. You definitely won't qualify for historical status now. *(Beat, looking downstage and out.)* You got a good wall for the Goya print right there.

(He glares.)

Don't glare. Early exposure to great art whets the appetite for life.

JACK

I'm thinking a bowl of fruit by Cezanne might work just as well.

EVELYN

(She sniffs.) I smell gas. You should open the windows, get some air in here. Your little stranger, when it arrives, will grow up with emphysema.

JACK

Our "little stranger" is not an "it", Ma, he's a boy. You're incredible.

And he's due in three weeks, so you have time to rehearse the nomenclature.

                              EVELYN

(*Pursed lips.*) You got a name picked out?

                               JACK

Mose.

                              EVELYN

Moses?

                               JACK

Not "Moses," just Mose. Mose Allen McIntyre-Evans.

                              EVELYN

(*Beat.*) Who's the "Allen" for?

                               JACK

The birth mother's last name is Allen, and since this is an open adoption and they will know each other—

                              EVELYN

Wai-wai-wait…open? What does that mean, anyone can join?

                               JACK

Ma—//

                              EVELYN

No, I'm seriously in the dark about these modern arrangements. This so-called birth mother, who from this point on you'll forgive me if I refer to as "B.M."…she's a clean, tax-paying citizen or a crack addict?

(*He crosses away.*)

Because if she's gonna be in your lives—//

JACK

I know what the problem is. You're pissed off because we're getting a live-in, not asking *you* to move in—//

EVELYN

I'm not pi—//

JACK

Because we didn't fix the basement up for your retire—//

EVELYN

I'm very happy in Sunrise!

(*Beat.*)

JACK

What do you want for lunch?

EVELYN

Oh, now...don't get all pinched. It's a lovely nursery and—//

JACK

Individual can of tuna on rye and a Cel-Ray okay?

EVELYN

You know I'm happy with anything. (*Another glare.*) So where's Tarzan?

JACK

Swinging from trees.

EVELYN

I never liked your sarcasm.

JACK

Ma! Look in the mirror!

EVELYN

No, no…that's your *paternal* gene pool.

> (*He laughs.*)

I'm dead serious. The few times I visited his crazy family in the
Bronx, they had me dissolved in tears within the first five minutes of
crossing the Whitestone Bridge. That Aunt Moira—//

JACK

(*Overlapping.*) Oh, please…not this—//

EVELYN

Go ahead and dis it, but it's the God's honest truth.

JACK

"Dis"? You're watching too much Oprah.

EVELYN

She's off!

JACK

She's syndicated!

> (*Ben has entered from above, a plastic Home Depot bag in
> hand.*)

BEN

Hello-o!

EVELYN

(*About-face.*) I LOVE THIS ROOM! Benny, you're a magician! And
that *bathroom*—! You've given me too much to kvell about...

JACK

(*He's had it.*) I'll get lunch started.

    (*Jack heads up to make lunch, leaving Evelyn and Ben to
    fawn.*)

BEN

So good to have you back, Evelyn. (*Air-kiss.*) Jack's been so excited.

EVELYN

Could have fooled me. I'm worried he's losing his sense of humor.

BEN

He's just preoccupied with fatherhood. It's a godsend. (*He sets out a
folding chair for her to sit on.*) How was your flight?

EVELYN

(*Sitting.*) These days, I'm just grateful the pilot's not drunk.

    (*Ben crosses to the crib box.*)

What's in the bag, ya big palooka?

BEN

A new set of Allen wrenches. I lent our neighbor the last set, which
he never returned, and the crib's from IKEA, Swedish. (*Reading
box.*) Actually, not Swedish, Swiss.

EVELYN

Better quality.

BEN

Yeah.

EVELYN

Bad neighbor.

BEN

Pete? Oh, he's alright. They're Evangelical Christians.

EVELYN

Oy, vey!

BEN

You've got your share of those in Florida, no?

EVELYN

More than our share! They hatch them in labs.

BEN

Pete's a good guy. They're followers of a British Evangelist, John Stott, who founded a very philanthropic and socially conscientious branch.

EVELYN

Another swami. You sound smitten.

BEN

Me? Nah. I just don't like to judge people before they're proven guilty.

EVELYN

Very New Testament of you. As long as you're not going all *Rosemary's Baby* on my Jacky.

(Evelyn heads left. Ben stops what he's doing and looks after her.)

BEN

How'dya mean?

EVELYN

(Evasive.) Ya got the stacking models I see.

BEN

Yeah, it was a space issue. Plus they're eco-friendly, so there was a tax incentive.

EVELYN

Whose idea was separates rather than attached?

BEN

Uh…Jack's?

EVELYN

Nice try. Jacky knows from appliances what I know from the internet. *(She tussles his hair.)* But he made a good catch in you, Mister Evans. Which is more than can be said for his Mamala.

BEN

No more Herbie?

EVELYN

Ugh, the schnorrer. On top of which, a player.

BEN

He's, like, eighty-six years old.

EVELYN

You think age is a corrective? Please. With the pills they got now,
even when an alter kocker's lying in his coffin his stiff pecker still
comes pokin' through the lid.

    (*Laughter.*)

I love what you're doing with the landscaping.

BEN

Good, no? We used decomposed granite to offset the agaves. Looks
like Mexico, doesn't it?

EVELYN

Better. Next time you're in Florida, I'll show you my lanai. I'm
putting in a little bonsai collection, but it needs someone with your
eye.

BEN

Bonsai? That's a helluva lot of work. (*Ribbing.*) You becoming a
connoisseur on us?

EVELYN

Hardly, I just like torturing living things into miniature versions of
themselves.

JACK (off)

(*Calling from above.*) Assemble the crib! Lunch is almost ready…

EVELYN

See what I mean? All work and no play makes Jack a dull boy.

BEN

The Shining.

EVELYN

What I'm saying. (*She shudders.*) Those twins!

BEN

Scare ya?

EVELYN

Enough to make me want to get my tubes tied. Though by then...
(*Shrugs.*)

BEN

Evelyn, when you said "go all *Rosemary's Baby* on Jacky," what did
you mean?

EVELYN

(*Indicating Jack.*) How's he doin', really?

    (*Beat. Ben doesn't have an answer. She eyes him closely.*)
Last year, when you moved in, my first visit...the Zoloft
prescription. All that meshuggah talk about a ghost in the house?
What was that about, you think?

BEN

Ancient history. He's been much better since the adoption went
through. He's off the meds and everything. We were pretty stressed
with the move.

EVELYN

No, Mr. Evans, Jacky was. You were cool as a cucumber. How

come?

BEN

I don't know. (*Beat.*) You ever been through an earthquake?

EVELYN

Please, these are new knees.

BEN

See, I like them. I mean, not the destruction or the casualties, but I grew up with them so when everything's actually shaking, I get kind of exhilarated. (*Beat. Embarrassed by admitting.*) I guess I find a loss of stability liberating.

EVELYN

That's what I worry about, Ben. Jacky's skittish enough as is. Oh, he's smart as they come, and accomplished in *his field*, and he's got the chutzpah to get whatever he sets his sights on…case in point. (*She gestures to him. Ben blushes.*) But ever since that boy was in booties, he's been susceptible to…to…how do I say this? (*Beat.*) Are you familiar with the term "dybbuk"?

BEN

I think so. It's Yiddish for a dead soul looking for a living host, right?

EVELYN

Bingo. I know this sounds nuts, and you can cart me off to cuckooville, *after* lunch, but Jacky's got one, a dybbuk, hovering. Always has, since he was this big. I don't know, maybe it was my fault. When my husband Perry died…he died right there, ya know, where you're putting the crib. Jacky was in his playpen, there. I was shopping. The worst day. I still blame myself for dawdling. Had I been here…after that, I never let him outta my sight. What do they call it now? Helicopter Mom? I was a B-52. "Overbearing" was the term we used to use. A single mom, you make mistakes. My sister said, "You're spoiling him!" At the time I thought, "That's okay, I'll transfer all the strength required of me for survival into this little boy." I'd stand, stern over those spilled Cheerios with my stiff finger in his face. "Eat!" Such big terrified eyes he had. Later, when they'd mock him and taunt him in school—why, because he was bright and cultured and a little sissified?—he'd come home with those same wide eyes, dilated, scared. Such a longing for protection. My heart couldn't handle two hurts—so I steeled myself for both our sakes. To be an example? What a mistake. Because honestly, the whole time? I was just so mad at his father for…jerk. Such a sensitive soul. The most tender person I'd ever met. I couldn't believe my luck. Smart, handsome, talented, funny, dead. Well, luck, if you haven't already figured this out, is never very permanent. A thousand pop songs will attest to that. Enough already. What's taking so long up there?

BEN

Evelyn…you just gave me a gift.

EVELYN

Yeah? Fat lotta good from this old trap, but whatever it was I hope it

311

helps. (*Point blank.*) Jacky's not easy, I guess we both know that. Always scared of…I-don't-know-what. Do you?

BEN

(*A rueful moment.*) I don't, but I think I've got a better picture now of what he struggles with. I love him, you know. When he's happy and focused with his eye on the positive, he's magnificent.

EVELYN

Good to hear. Still…as a parent you know too much. (*Beat.*) Maybe, when I lost that twin of his— (*Big sigh.*) My sister should have never told him.

> (*Startled by this, Ben's about to ask more when a large crash comes from upstairs. Jack enters, distraught. Ben rushes to him.*)

BEN

What happened? You okay? Jack, what happened?

JACK

The agency just called. The birth mother's keeping the baby. She tore up the contract.

> (*Lights fade.*)

Scene 2

(*Same room, late that night. Mozart's Piano Sonata #11 playing on child's boom box. Lights slowly up on Jack, seated down left on a child's stool, quietly crying, a small teddy bear in his hands, a tiny penguin shirt on his lap. A bottle of vodka sits on the floor next to him. The unassembled crib still in its box. After a long beat, lights come up and Ben appears at the top of the stairs, in pajama bottoms, open robe.*)

BEN

Hey. It's late. What are you doing down there in the dark?

JACK

I'm sitting alone in the dark.

BEN

(*Grabbing a folding chair to sit beside him.*) Want company?

JACK

Why, who's here?

BEN

Nobody but us chickens. (*He sits.*)

JACK

(*Exaggerated, sloppy.*) You'll *alwaysh* be *ch-ch-chicken* to me. (*He reaches down for the vodka.*)

BEN

Whoa, whoa, whoa, not straight out of the bottle—

JACK

Okay. Not. (*He puts the bottle back down. Very soberly.*) How was that visit for you?

BEN

Your mother? Good.

JACK

You got an earful. Rhapsody in *Jew*. (*He clicks off the music.*)

BEN

She was great with me. Not you?

JACK

Between the loathsome sneer and her affectionate term for the birth mother…thank God her Brandeis Alumni group booked themselves into the Ritz-Carlton. You'd be pulling me off her decapitated corpse right now.

BEN

Wow, decapitation. I wouldn't have taken you for the scimitar type.

JACK

Scimitar?! Fuck that…WITH MY BARE TEETH!

 (*Stubbornly, Jack swigs from the bottle. A silent beat.*)

So what now, Benjamin Evans?

BEN

We reapply.

JACK

Not sure I've got it in me.

BEN

(*Beat.*) You mean that?

JACK

I don't know. Did I say it?

BEN

You've been so on point all year, Jack. Totally motivated and practical about every aspect of adopting, even more so than me. Don't get cold feet now. This is just a speed bump.

> (*Jack is silent. Beat.*)

Evelyn mentioned something to me today…about a twin? Your lost twin.

JACK

(*Throws arms up.*) Christ, that old wives' tale. When the hell did she—//

BEN

Today, while you were making lunch. Did you know about—//

JACK

I heard all about it from my crazy Aunt Rose. She's just fuckin' with you.

BEN

Why would she?

315

JACK

My mother was the youngest of six. She was teased mercilessly.
Consider her the abused sibling who grows up with a penchant for
abuse.

BEN

Well, okay. But it's weird. She said she was pregnant with twins and
then—

JACK

Ben, *back off*! You think I offed my own twin in utero? It's like a
tabloid headline: "MYSTERIOUS TWIN CONSUMED BY
RAVENOUS BROTHER—*BEFORE BIRTH!*" I may be a carnivore
but…why don't we look at it this way? Maybe I'm just not fit to
adopt.

BEN

(*Sincerely.*) Right. (*Beat.*) Maybe it's just the univ—//

JACK

Don't blame the universe, please. There's no intergalactic message in
this, Ben. Heather Allen wants her kid. He gets to stay with her. It's a
great thing, really. He'll have his mother directly in his life, and with
any luck, he'll mature in a healthy environment surrounded by loads
of *biological* affection…and love. Nature vs. nurture, whoopee!
Which maybe is, after all, what was intended when whoever the fuck
conceived this world set it spinning. I don't know, if it was up to me,
would I want a neurotic gay man like me raising my kid?

BEN

Two gay men. Of course you would. You gotta cut all this self-loathing out, Jack. You're the most beautiful man I know. Own it, will ya?

(*Jack's unconvinced.*)

C'mon. Take a breath. Look at the support we've got now.

(*Jack starts to protest.*)

No, I'm serious. Look how far we've come. If we don't live up to the last fifty years of LGBT progress—//

JACK

And what? Risk bringing up a child in this still-all-too-bigoted world, exposing him to what we deal with every day? Need I remind you who lives across the street? Get real, Ben. The Glorias are legion. The Heather Allens have won.

(*Ben rises.*)

At least in this scenario, at a not-too-distant point in little Mose's development he might be self-assured and independent enough to step out on his own and individuate, followed by the requisite period of resentment and inevitable decapitation of the mother with his canine incisors—MOSE, *NOW* YOU ARE A MAN! (*Weepy, reaching to swig.*) I really liked "Mose." She'll probably name him something common, like Cooper or Conner... (*Sitting, he takes another pull of alcohol.*)

BEN

(*He's been packing toys, but turns fierce.*) Okay, enough now. Stop it! I'm not going to indulge in this with you anymore. (*Pulls bottle away from Jack.*)

JACK

(*Taken aback.*) Indulge? In what?//

BEN

Self-pity. Enough! You're not the only one who's lost out here—

JACK

Thus spake the alcoholic's son. (*Off Ben's look.*) Sorry. I know that you lost out, too—//

BEN

Yeah, you know, and still the pity party: "Boo-hoo-hoo, it's all about me! What *I* lost." Well, I'm sorry you're feeling so porous, Jack—//

JACK

Porous? Who said I was—//

BEN

(*Exploding.*) Goddamn it! For once, will you let me goddamn feel what I goddamn feel and not have to nurse *you* through it? For *once?!*

(*Beat. Jack is flabbergasted. Ben begins packing away various baby items.*)

JACK

This isn't very Episcopalian of you, Ben.

BEN

(*Turning fierce.*) No, you know why? Because I got *real* kids right now in my classroom with some real issues—

JACK

(*His hackles up.*) "Real" issues—?

BEN

Not enough money for lunch, Jack. That's real. Dad's out of work for two years and just broke Johnny's jaw. Thirteen-year-old Laneesha can't hold her head up for more than five minutes since her older brother taught her how to huff. And little Juan? Little Juan from Guatemala has been sleeping at the railyard since his illegal parents got picked up and deported. Yeah, I think those trump our first failed pass at adoption.

JACK

I just love it when your halo starts to glow.

> (*Beat. Ben is dumbstruck. Without uttering another word, he bounds upstairs. Jack, regretful, picks up a small teddy bear, speaks to it.*)

Once upon a time there was a little boy who really didn't know who he was. (*Then, with new clarity…*) Let me rephrase that. He didn't know what *being a "he"* was. His father had left the picture so early, you see, so he never really got initiated. Instead, the little boy impersonated his mother, thinking that if he did it well enough, the rest would take care of itself. This was a long time after Stonewall, so no one really noticed outside the schoolyard where the "HE-boys" ruled, or if they did, well…there were plenty just like him in the wider world who seemed to be making lotsa progress: Ellen Degeneres, Anderson Cooper. And so he went about finding a husband, a house… (*À la Streisand.*) …and a beautiful reflection…and soon, he was swollen with child. But one day, just when his baby was ready for delivery he found that, lo and behold, there was nowhere for it to come out. No part of him could open that wide. Thus it lived and grew *inside* him, the baby did…forever and ever…amen. (*Beat.*) So now what the fuck do we do?

> (*The distant sound of neighborhood dogs barking, quickly followed by a strong rumble as a high-magnitude earthquake hits. Things crash, shelves collapse, Jack falls off the stool. Ben stumbles down the staircase, trying to maintain his equilibrium, but falls, too.*)

BEN

JACK! JACK!

> (*Dust falls from the ceiling as the sounds of everything in the house above them crashing, breaking sustains—a cacophony of car alarms, dogs—finally, the shaking subsides, and as the sounds die down…*)

JACK	BEN
Shit!	Awesome!

(*Blackout.*)

Scene 3

(Same basement, next morning. Sound of static. Lights up on the room lit by a halogenic camper lamp only, on floor. There are four folding chairs. Seated in two of them are PETE, 50s, and FRANCINE, 40, the Evangelicals from next door, in sweats. Ben is fiddling with radio until he gets reception—an official voice being broadcast.)

MAYOR (V.O.)

"...last night, at approximately 3:56am, we sustained a massive temblor, 7.1 magnitude, the epicenter being somewhere in the eastern part of— *(Static.)* Large portions of the county remain without power, water, or emergency services. We have no idea the extent of injury or loss in human life at this time, with only one reported fatality.

(Pete and Francine bow heads, hold hands as if to pray. Out of respect, Ben reaches for the radio.)

The President has dispatched the army reserves, and FEMA is already on the ground evaluating property damages...

(Ben shuts off the radio and puts it aside as Jack descends into the basement holding a tray with another camper light, mugs, CoffeeMate. Ben signals him not to interrupt.)

PETE

(*Head still bowed, eyes closed.*) …and we pray, sweet Jesus, for the immediate passage of this catastrophe's first soul, released out of mayhem, and for all those who may, in the days to come, be set free of this veil of tears, to find their humble way to your welcoming embrace. For Thine is the Kingdom and the Glory…

FRANCINE

Praise the Way.

> (*Jack moves forward as if to serve some coffee, but Ben shoots him a look that stops him.*)

PETE

And finally, for otherwise his arms will give out on him, to these beautiful brothers, Ben and Jake—

JACK

(*Sotto voce.*) Jack.

> (*Ben scowls.*)

PETE

—whose strength of character and loving concern have made it possible for them to accept us, your humble servants, Pete and Francine, having lost our own dear bungalow and suffered great ruin. This act we attribute to you, Dear Lord…

> (*Jack attempts to serve the coffee again, but Pete's not quite done.*)

Yea, though we walk through this valley of sorrow, we pause here to acknowledge *this* house of love, and the generosity, the neighborliness, the selflessness, the kindness of Ben, of Jake—

JACK

Jack. (*Giving up, cheerful.*) Who wants cold Nescafé?!

PETE & FRANCINE

Praise the Way! Amen.

> (*They bow heads, touch. Francine begins to sob on Pete's shoulder. Jack motions to Ben to come round to his side and help, and he does, spooning Nescafé into one mug at a time and passing them out.*)

BEN

(*Gently to Pete*) Does she take it black or…?

FRANCINE

(*Through tears.*) Stevia or Splenda and some one-percent milk?

> (*Ben looks to Jack who shakes his head, no. She understands.*)

Just black is fine.

JACK

(*Too buoyant.*) Oh, good, because our fridge has passed out on the kitchen floor and with no electricity…well, there's Coffee-Mate—Tra-la!

PETE

I'll take Coffee-Mate. Thanks so much.

> (*As Ben hands him a mug.*)

And after coffee, Ben, if you like, I'm happy to go upstairs with you and right that fridge. I'm guessing it's a two-man job.

BEN

Jeez, Pete. (*Apologetic.*) Excuse me—okay to say "jeez"?

PETE

It's okay, He loves to be called by his names.

FRANCINE

(*Somewhat recovered thanks to coffee.*) Praise the Ways!

BEN

What I was going to say is sure, I'm happy to actually…honestly, I don't know how to say thanks. (*Still with Pete.*) You positive you're up for…?

PETE

Aw, Ben, I can't tell you how important it is for me to apply myself to something useful right now. And righting your refrigerator is a fine start.

> (*Jack finally sets the tray down, shaking blood back into his hands.*)

JACK

(*Sitting.*) May I just say—it's Jack by the way, not Jake—

PETE & FRANCINE

(*Smiling at him.*) Hi, Jack!

JACK

Uh…may I just say that I'm really sad to see the devastation your house sustained? I know we haven't had any contact to speak of before this, and I feel really shitty—*bad* about that, but I want you to know that I have always admired the care you two put into the upkeep of your place, and, to be perfectly frank…what the hell were you feeding those roses?

(*Francine dissolves in tears again.*)

Oh, crap…I'm sorry. Did I put my foot in it again?

FRANCINE

(*Sucking it up.*) I'm okay! I'm okay! Don't censor yourself. We're not that…you know, fussy.

JACK

No?

FRANCINE

Oh, no. In fact, I've always felt awful that I haven't been more aggressive myself—not aggressive *per se*, that's not the right word—*forthcoming,* and just made my way over to bring you some Bundt cake or homemade pumpkin pie.

JACK

I do love pumpkin pie.

FRANCINE

You do?!

JACK

Oh, yeah. Ben doesn't, do you, Ben?

(*Ben shakes his head adamantly.*)

It reminds him of earwax. But I'm from back east and I just love—//

FRANCINE

(*As though it's Valhalla.*) Oh, back east! How cool is that? I also make an amazing Boston cream!

JACK

That not so much.

>   (*As Jack and Francine schmooze up a storm, Pete puts his mug down and signals Ben, and together they head upstairs.*)

FRANCINE

Oh, mine you'd like. I use Spanish Madeira and grenadine whipped right into the heavy cream, and on top—shaved dark chocolate, 70%…

JACK

Stop! It sounds amazing.

FRANCINE

Yep, it is! (*Innuendo plus.*) I can get Pete to do just about *anything* when I serve *that* for dessert.

JACK

Anything?

FRANCINE

(*Suggestively.*) Yep. (*Beat.*)

JACK

(*Coloring.*) Francine! You're making me blush.

>   (*She giggles. He giggles.*)

Where are *you* from?

FRANCINE

Lorain, Ohio.

JACK

Huh, the Rust Bowl. (*He sits beside her.*) That's a pretty depressed
area now, isn't it? Economically.

FRANCINE

Oh, yes. Always been, really. Steel and coal used to make it viable,
back when there was manufacturing there. Now, *pft!*— flatlined. Still
got a kid brother who's there—Eddy—divorced, unemployed,
medicated. A couple of nieces, too, but…once you get out of Lorain,
you're gone for good, believe me. Lake Erie's just a sludge pit of
chemicals now. Shame.

> (*She smiles at him, sweetly. He follows suit. Is she flirting?*
>
> *Meantime, a loud thud is heard above, and cheers.*)

(*She sings from Frank Sinatra's "High Hopes."*) "Whoops, there
goes another rubber tree plant." (*Laughs, embarrassed.*)

JACK

Funny, everyone I've ever known who's originally from Ohio has
a great sense of humor.

FRANCINE

Mm-hm. Cleveland, mostly, right?

JACK

Why is that?

FRANCINE

(*Shrugs.*) Best you can do with adversity, I guess.

JACK

Oh. Well, I'm not a glass-half-full kind of person.

FRANCINE

You could have fooled me.

JACK

Really?

FRANCINE

I think you guys are grand.

JACK

(*Beat.*) Francine…you and Pete know that we're…?

FRANCINE

Oh, we don't care about that!

JACK

You know what I was going to—//

FRANCINE

(*Putting mug down.*) You're gay.

JACK

Right.

FRANCINE

And very beautiful. We both think so. Especially here…

(*She touches his chest and he reacts like a jolt has hit him.*)

Sorry. Can I ask you something?

JACK

As long as it's not, "Which one's the girl?"

FRANCINE

(*She laughs.*) No. (*Beat*). Are you guys adopting?

JACK

(*Rising.*) Oh, my God…

(*A small aftershock rumbles, sending some dust down on them. She scrambles to the floor and he under a chair. The rumble subsides. From above, Ben calls.*)

BEN (off)

You two okay?

JACK

We're fine! (*To her.*) You fine?

(*She nods.*)

We're fine! You?

BEN (off)

We're good. (*To Pete.*) Pete, would you sweep up that glass? (*To Jack.*) Your mother's Goya print didn't make it.

JACK

(*Unable to control it.*) Praise the Way! (*Turning to Francine.*) So, where were we?

(*She pats her tummy.*)

Oh, yeah. Why did you ask if we're adopting?

FRANCINE

(*Gesturing at the obvious.*) All this baby stuff…

JACK

Right. Well, we were all set to go…three weeks away, and yesterday someone had a change of heart.

FRANCINE

Ben?

JACK

Birth mom.

FRANCINE

(*Nods knowingly.*) They can do that.

JACK

She did.

FRANCINE

(*Beat.*) We can't.

JACK

Adopt or conceive?

FRANCINE

(*She gets up to inspect the crib.*) The latter. Don't mention I told you, but Pete got a staph infection from bad clams. He's infertile. I still wish, but…

JACK

There are lots of alternative methods if you're patient and determined. Listen to me, I sound like Dr. Phil.

FRANCINE

It's a fortune, and right now…our living situation is, well, compromised.

JACK

(*Beat.*) Francine…do you and Pete ever worry that you're never going to last as a couple if you don't…you know, have—

FRANCINE

Offspring?

JACK

Yeah.

FRANCINE

There are always miracles. Who knows? (*Cautiously.*) Maybe some surrogate someone… (*Smiles, shrugs.*) But if it doesn't happen…well, we took vows.

JACK

Oh yeah, those. 'Til recently only straight people got to take those.

FRANCINE

Sorry. That was unseemly of me. I forget sometimes we've had privileges you don't.

JACK

May I remind you that it's thanks to fundamentalist Christians mostly that our privileges have been provisional?

(*He begins tidying, picking up trays, cups.*)

FRANCINE

We're a much more tolerant sect than most.

JACK

(*Slamming tray down—a sharp retort.*) Tolerant? You tolerate a sore throat, Francine. You tolerate mosquito bites. What gives you, a heterosexual white woman of means and privilege, any right to *tolerate* anybody? It's demeaning. Take it from the frequently demeaned.

FRANCINE

Yes. I understand. (*She starts to exit, but pauses, turns back.*) May I tell you something? (*A change has come over her. She strides back.*) I used to be a showgirl in Vegas.

JACK

Wow, *that* was not on my shopping cart.

FRANCINE

Oh, yeah. From six years old I had one ambition—to be a Rat Pack Copa Girl. (*Straightens her spine, chest out.*) "Good evening, Mr. Sinatra…"

> (*Strutting, arms wide, she sings a bar of "Blues in the Night."*)

"My mama done told me, UH. (*Hip thrust.*) When I was in pigtails, UH. My mama done told me, Hon…"

> (*Stops.*)

Not bad, huh? So I quit high school, hopped a bus to Nevada. I was sixteen. Well, that old dream Vegas was long gone, but I thought, "At least let me try out for Wayland Flowers' 'Madame Goes to Harlem' show—" but he was dead, too. So I wound up backing up RuPaul at a porn star convention, and none too soon, I found my way to the heart of old Las Vegas. It's not onstage or backstage…it's right out there, front of house. No my dear, it ain't show business. It's *blow* business. And let me tell you, it was *lu-cra-tive.* Money, money, money. The high rollers were still everywhere—sexy and mean! And when the stakes get higher the players get meaner. Some of them like nothing better than coking up the help—young, pretty, *female* help, just for the sport of it. They'd tally up the carnage like hunters with a roof-load of twelve-point deer swilling rot-gut coffee 'round the gas pump. Ever seen a coke addict two years into the dream? Not pretty. I just couldn't get the color back in my cheeks. Pinch, pinch, pinch—no luck. So, eventually, I was demoted to Keno Girl for the breakfast buffet crowd. But the damn bloody noses wouldn't stop, so…I got ushered right out the emergency exit one pink Vegas dawn with a bad habit, no credit…one whole day I sat on the filthy asphalt by this big stinking dumpster, no clue what to do. That's where Pete found me. My French-tipped manicure bit right down to the cuticles. Holes in my fishnets. Dried blood all caked down my…dear Pete. He was so tolerant with my drying out. An angel. "For what is it if you gain the world and lose your soul?" Matthew, 16:26. You see, I'm acquainted with tolerance.

JACK

Wow…and now you've lost your home.

FRANCINE

But we have each other, and we have our faith. You might try adding some of that to *your* way of life—just a pinch. Faith is a real nice condiment.

JACK

Praise the Way?

FRANCINE

His Way. Or another way, more…your *own* way. A couple shouldn't have to rely on themselves alone to build a house that'll last forever.

(*Suddenly there are loud shouts from above.*)

BEN (off)

(*Calling.*) HEY, JACK! Pete found some stuff back behind the fridge where the wall cracked open, looks to be pretty interesting.

JACK

(*To Ben.*) I hope it's my Mother's Japanese "happi coat." (*To Francine.*) She lost it on her first visit last year and insists I gave it to Goodwill.

(*Ben comes bounding down with Pete, who's holding a bunting full of children's toys including a very dusty teddy bear.*)

BEN

Look at all this—it's vintage kid stuff.

(*Jack recognizes the teddy bear, a dark look coming over his face.*)

JACK

That's my Dah-bah.

BEN

Your what?

JACK

My dah— (*He stops himself and quickly recoils.*)

BEN

Jack...you recognize this. Was it—//

JACK

(*Blanching.*) I don't know what that shit is. It's junk. Throw it away.

PETE

Wait a second, there's a date embroidered on this blanket.
(*Squinting.*) It's hard to make out. See, there it is. (*Brushing dust.*)
August 7th, 19...

FRANCINE

(*Squinting.*) ...78.

BEN

Jack, that's your birthday.

(*Ben moves to touch him, but reflexively, Jack skitters away.*)

JACK

Don't, Ben. Don't.

(*He crosses down left, takes out his cellphone, dials.*)

Meanwhile…)

PETE

(*Of the bundle.*) I'm just going to put all this down here… (*Places the bundle down center.*) Francine, would you join me please?

(*She does. They kneel together to pray, Ben watching Jack.*)

(*Pete and Francine bow their heads silently as…lights fade.*)

PETE	JACK
We thank you, Divine Spirit, for what we have recovered in this house today. May it foretell recoveries yet to come.	(*On cell.*) Dr. Frielich, this is your former patient, Jack McIntyre. Would you get back to me ASAP? I need to refill that expired prescription for Zoloft…"

Scene 4

(Two days hence. The basement nursery. Ben is stacking packed boxes stage left, labeled FOR GOODWILL, FOR FEMA, FOR MIDGE + LAMBSHANKS, talking on a cellphone, a box of clothes nearby. Meanwhile, from above, the muffled sounds of a TV morning talk show.)

BEN

(On cellphone.) …right…I see…right…thanks a lot, Evelyn…oh yeah yeah yeah, we're fine. A little damage, not extensive… electricity's back. How'd your knees hold up? …good. Well, I'm glad your plane took off…no. These two days since have been…trying. Hold on one sec— *(He mutes his phone and calls upstairs.)* JACK?! *(To phone again.)* Sorry, I thought I heard him moving around but I think he's still knocked out…pretty shook up, but…I'm sure…alright, I'll have him call you…okay, bye.

(He puts the phone in his pocket, turns his attention back to the boxes. We hear the door at the top of the stairs open and Jack's manic voice.)

JACK (off)

You should fuckin' see this, Ben. Rosanne Barr is on talking about her plastic surgery. She looks like Faye Dunaway now. *(Crazy laugh.)* It's so confusing. Renee Zellweger looks like Robin Wright

337

looks like Jessica Lange looks like Caitlyn Jenner. Insanity. I want to look like Taylor Swift!

(*Sound of the door closing.*)

BEN

(*To himself.*) Jesus Christ.

(*Ben, exasperated, tries to continue working. Beat. The door above opens again.*)

JACK (off)

Oh my God! BEN! COME UP HERE! THIS IS A *SCREAM!* They're about to talk to a Doctor of Chinese Medicine about the health benefits of "Tantric Sex"!

(*Ben has had it. He rushes to the foot of the stairs, bellowing.*)

BEN

SHUT IT OFF!

JACK (off)

What? I'm watching Hulu—

BEN

JACK! Shut your goddamned laptop and come down here, right now!

(*We hear footsteps to and footsteps fro, and Jack descends. He wears a huge terrycloth bathrobe and bunny slippers.*)

We can't keep this up. We're in two worlds. You, spending all day up there in those *slippers*, watching bullshit. And me, down here packing up all this…shit, like something good is happening still. But it's not. Nothing good is happening. What's real, Jack? Answer me.

(*Jack shifts uneasily. Long beat.*)

You gonna say anything?

JACK

(*Dissembling.*) I saw a PBS special on artificial insemination.

BEN

Uh-huh…

JACK

It was interesting.

BEN

Pertinent to this discussion?

JACK

Could be. Theoretically.

BEN

No. No, I can't process any more theoreticals, Jack.

JACK

We've been through some—//

BEN

Some traumas, I know. But we're either alive and moving forward, *together*, in the here and now, or we're rolling over and playing dead in front of Hulu. Which?

(*Silence.*)

(*Reasonably now.*) From day one you intuited this chaos. *You* did.

I've been in denial. Now can we please help each other face the crazy unresolved shit that took place in this house so that—//

JACK

So that I can be the perfect little wife.

BEN

(*Fierce.*) Stop fucking finishing my sentences. (*Beat.*) Jack, we had four years of unqualified bliss that led us to believe we could do this. (*Gestures to surroundings.*) But look at us. Here we are, buried in the basement hating the look of each other. The last year has been nothing but trials, since day one. We thought we could do that, too… (*Points to crib box.*) *I* did, anyway. And now, all that's left is… (*Gestures to pile of boxes.*) So tell me—it's up to you now—you can stay stuck in your victimhood or you can go on living life with me. Which?

JACK

I'm numb, that's all.

BEN

I'm not! Feel something! (*He grabs Jack's hand and puts it on his chest.*) Can you feel *this?* Can you?

JACK

(*Calmly.*) Now you're being abusive, Ben. (*Violently pulling away.*) Let go.

BEN

Fine. (*Letting go.*) Okay. (*Stepping away.*) Okay. (*He picks up his keys.*) I'm letting go. (*Moving to stairs.*)

JACK

Where you going?

BEN

Out. I don't know where. I'm going driving.

JACK

When will you be back?

(*Ben just looks at him.*)

You going cruising?

BEN

Jesus.

JACK

You can, you know. There's that spot down by the viaduct—//

BEN

Cut it out.

JACK

You could pick up one of the day laborers out in front of Home Depot—it'll cost you, but you like dark meat.

BEN

What are you doing?

JACK

I don't mind. We're not fucking *each other* lately, you're too busy down here playing Daddy all day.

(*In a fury, Ben finds something to break and breaks it. Jack is*

341

taken aback for a moment, then recovers. Ben steps back.)

BEN

Satisfied?

JACK

Nice. So all bets are off, I guess.

(*Ben looks away.*)

I thought we were *forever*, Ben. That was the bottom line, wasn't it?
No matter what?

(*Silence.*)

Would you like to chime in?

BEN

I've said enough. I don't know what else you want me to say, Jack.

JACK

Fuck you! Why don't you try saying that. And if that's too David
Mamet then come up with your own damn dialogue. Say something
honest that I don't have to come up with for you.

BEN

(*Angering.*) Something honest?

JACK

Yeah.

BEN

Alright. Your Father dropped dead right there. (*Pointing to spot.*)
With you in the playpen beside him. Talk to your Mother about it.
She'll confirm it. And you *did* have a twin. She lost it in the first

trimester. Flushed out in a rush of blood. She thought she'd lost both of you, but no…*you* survived. (*Realizing.*) I see it now…that's why you freak out at the idea of a kid. You're too fucked up to live with *anybody*.

JACK

What a crock o' shit. The two of you are psychoanalyzing me now? You'd better listen to me, Ben…just because your capacity to tolerate my black moods has all but extinguished itself, don't think—

BEN

FUCK YOU!

JACK

THERE WE GO!

BEN

YOU CAN GO FUCK YOURSELF, JACK!

JACK

I'D GET A LOT MORE THRILL THAN I GET OUT OF YOUR LIMP PRICK! YOU SAVING THE *BIG STIFFIE* FOR PETE NEXT DOOR?! GO FOR IT! FINALLY, YOU GET TO FUCK YOUR DADDY!

> (*Enraged, Ben charges him and for a moment it's an all-out tussle as they roll about the floor, Ben quickly gaining the upper hand. Just as he is winding back his arm for a blow, he stops himself. Totally winded. Ben gets up, rights himself— long beat—Jack remains seated. They're breathing hard. Ben*

343

moves to a far end of the room. Beat.)

We should never have bought this house. Fucking "forever house."
Yeah, right. All we've done is bury ourselves in it. In debt, and in
every other way. It's just come down to entrapment. And a fucking
quake. The walls moving...the walls! But the truth is they've been
moving all year, Ben. Closing us in and crushing us like some bad
Roger Corman movie. And we bought into it. This isn't a home, it's a
tomb. Well, hooray, 'cause now it's our tomb. Our great big fucking
mausoleum. So, yeah, go. Let's just bury the whole enterprise while
we can, shall we? I'll set fire to the place. Here lies Jack and Ben.
Burn in hell!

> (*He covers his face with his hands. A long beat. Finally*
> *bucking up.*)

I always knew you would leave me.

BEN

Jesus Christ, Jack...confront your fucking demons. Please. I can't do
it for you. (*He crosses down to retrieve the box of clothes he's giving*
away.) I'm dropping the rest of these clothes off for Pete and
Francine. FEMA's got them holed up at the Holiday Inn...and you
should know, they're eager to talk to us...

JACK

About?

BEN

Turkey basters and Dixie cups. (*Heading for the stairs.*)

344

JACK

Ben!

BEN

(*He halts again.*) Will you let me go?

JACK

(*Not quite resolute.*) I'm gonna change.

BEN

(*Big sigh.*) I wish you meant it.

> (*He's gone. Jack is distraught, stumbles around not knowing where to turn. Then his eyes come to rest on the corner where his father died, and he is spellbound. He begins picking up after Ben and in the process crosses to an open box containing his Dah-bah teddy. Beat.*)

JACK

Damnit, I can do this. I can...

> (*He reaches down placing both hands on the teddy, squeezing his eyes shut. With a deep breath, he lifts the imaginary baby that the bear now represents—the rest is to Dah-bah.*)

Hey, Dah-bah. Wake up, little guy. You were here when all this shit started. We're in this together, pal. You and me. Come on...let's take a crack at it...you be Mose and...I'll be Daddy.

> (*He carries the teddy in his arms toward center stage, then holds it out in front to address it. Note: At some point during*

345

Jack's upcoming address, Ben quietly appears above,
unseen.)

First off, there's a few things we gotta get *straight,* so to speak, before we take this *Daddy* thing any further. I don't do amusement parks. Maybe Magic Mountain, when you're *thirty.* But not Disneyland. Ever. You're going to have to rely on aunts and uncles and high school friends for that. Life here is going to be amusing enough. Now…

(*He sits with Dah-bah center, continuing to talk to it.*)
About life here…there are some funny things you'll need to know about "Daddy"… (*Putting the Dah-bah on his lap and affecting a German dialect.*) Let me show you how Daddy *spricht* "amusement park."

(*Suddenly—Lights! Music! Stage is transformed into a*
fantastic amusement park with a sign overhead:
"GAYLAND". Jack is amazed.)

WILLKOMMEN TO GAYLAND!

(*He decides to go with the magical spirit of it all.*)
Come, *mein Kind,* step right this way! Put on those ruby slippers, babe. You're on the ground floor of Gayland, where all queer Daddies WORSHIP DIVAS!

(*Sound of "Over the Rainbow," or some disco rave music.*
Note: To visually enhance "Gayland," projections may be
useful. Or all this might work as well in the imaginary realm.)

346

See, that's Judy, Barbra, Madge, Gaga, Beyoncé, and a few lesser deities like Britney and—

(*Francine enters in full showgirl regalia, dances a few steps to "Blues in the Night."*)

Pretty, huh?

(*Suddenly, Francine is wobbling, having snorted too much coke.*)

Don't touch the holograms!

(*She exits.*)

Now follow the yellow brick road…and poof! We're in Grey Gardens, where all movie trivia goes to die! No, that's not Grandma, that's "Baby Jane"—yes, Joan Crawford played her sister, good guess! Look, Divine! And who's that polishing off the Pink Flamingo? Yessiree, it's John Waters! Oh, honey, let me tell you, Daddy sure has killed time here sorting through esoteric bullshit. In the shadow? What shadow? You mean from *Brokeback Mountain*?! No, that's just the story of two men scared of being outed. Oh, yeah…we're everywhere. Sure, plenty of celebrities, too. I know, peanut, Gayland's very crowded and sometimes it gets overcast. Maybe that's why Daddy gets so grouchy. OR MAYBE IT'S BECAUSE, WHEN HE WAS FOURTEEN, HE WAS JUMPED BY A GANG ON THE PLAYGROUND: "What are you looking at, faggot? You never learned how to make a fist? Where's your mommy, bitch boy?" (*Recovering.*) BUT why cry over spilt milk?

Look! Here's a patch of sunshine! It's Toys for Twinks! Where all our early tendencies are revealed! Ready? A little preference test…which would you rather hold, Barbie or that football? The doll? Chip off the old block! I think you're ready for a stroll down memory lane…this is the LGBT-prequel, babe. That history lesson Daddy Ben encouraged…look! Backless chaps and crotchless candy underpants! Twenty-five cent porn arcades! Glory holes and amyl vials! Dark parks, crowded piers, bathroom stalls, bareback orgies and the ever popular all-night hustle…uh-oh, don't go too far back. They're filling up paddy wagons that way.

(*Sings Martha and the Vandellas' "Nowhere to Run."*)
"Nowhere to run, nowhere to hide…"

(*Stops.*)

Whaddaya say we get off the streets and bring it all back home…why, just look what's on the internet now: an M4M Chat Room…oh, Brave New World—we've entered the present— ManHub, Grindr, Zoosk.com—no, no, do not touch. "Parental Advisory." Still, something wicked this way comes…

(*Suddenly, Bill appears dressed menacingly as a leather daddy. Jack coddles Dah-bah protectively as Bill exits. Continues with mounting urgency.*)

NO! Two steps forward, one step back…a generation back. Just follow the Village People past the YMCA to the sign that says "Protected"—no, not *"Infected"*! You'll wind up in Plagueville—oh, you see, sweetie. Now we gotta ACT UP, 'cause "Silence = Death" in Plagueville. It's not getting any easier, is it? Don't freak. Join the marches for gay pride, on WeHo! On Washington! Woo-hoo! Cocktails with Obama on the White House lawn! We're living now, ain't we? Defying life expectancies. What do you mean, "still second class citizens"? We got the 14th Amendment. We got marriage in fifty states! Americans won't stand for...won't stand for what? Equality for queers? Fast forward! Roll the Matthew Shepard tape! Screen *Boys Don't Cry*! I hear that in Nigeria they like their fags well-hung, as in lynching and castrating. Face it, we're universally reviled! Putin's passed a Hate Bill. And who knows what can turn around here...

(*Turning on the Dah-bah.*)

What's the matter, bitch-boy? You don't like being reviled? I said FACE IT! We'll *always* be reviled! Make a fist, damnit. No one ever taught you? Where's your daddy, faggot? I'll teach you...

(*Jumping up, he throws the Dah-bah down in a fury.*)

And that's exactly why I don't feel fit to be your father. (*Coming to terms.*) "Unfit to be a father." ...aw, shit...

(*As sounds and projections of Gayland fade and lights restore, he drops the game. Beat. He looks down at the teddy again—can he do this? Yes.*)

"Confront your fucking demons, Jack." That's what he said. Okay. Let's try a new approach...

(*With his eyes now focused where his own father died, down right…*)

Come on, little one. Time to make a visit to a gravesite…

(*He picks Dah-bah up, tenderly carries it right and settles down among the remnants of a child's world. Beat. Hugging Dah-bah.*)

Come to Papa…

(*Jack begins to sing Gershwin's "Embraceable You" with great resolve.*)

"Don't be a naughty baby. Come to Papa, come to Papa do…my sweet embraceable…"

(*Squeezing his eyes shut and the bear to his chest, he begins to recover the memory of that fateful day. Mounting primal scream.*)

Dah-bah…Dah-bah…DAAAH-BAAAAAAAH!!! (*Spent, he lowers his head.*)

(*Ben, having witnessed all this, stealthily moves down the stairs and touches Jack's shoulder. A jolt as Jack blinks back to the here and now. He tries to pull himself together. Awkward beat.*)

How much of that did you see?

BEN

Enough.

(*Crossing left to put Dah-bah back.*) I didn't do all that well, I'm afraid.

BEN

Yeah, you did.

JACK

I…just…took a swipe at it.

BEN

A big swipe.

(*Jack is about to protest.*)

Shh…

(*Holds up a finger, recites.*)

"That's what happens when ghosts get into the house. They try to frighten you with their beckoning fingers and clanking chains, not knowing that they're dead…they're dead…"

(*Retrieves the rest of "Design for Living."*)

"…they're dead…and unable to harm you anymore. That's why one should never be scared of them. Poor little ghosts! It must be so uncomfortable, wandering through empty passages, feeling they're not wanted very much."

(*Jack has settled on the floor listening.*)

JACK

I don't want ghosts in our house anymore, Ben. I want you and me.

(*Ben nods, touches Jack's face, they hug.*)

I'm so sorry…

BEN

And I'm sorry I pushed you so hard so fast.

> (*Finally Jack frees himself from the hug, dead serious.*)

JACK

Ben…if my twin had survived…stronger, smarter, sane and straighter…

BEN

I still would have chosen you.

JACK

It's you, you know…who makes me happy. Long as I got that, bring on the kids. (*Looking around.*) Unpack these boxes. (*Beat.*) Marry me, Ben.

BEN

Have you eaten anything today?

JACK

Some pride, I think. And you know what? It went down good.

BEN

Seriously, you're the one who always had a problem with getting married—//

JACK

Fuck that. Just say I do.

BEN

(*Beat.*) I'm not sure.

352

JACK

Come on… (*Kneeling.*) Will you marry me?

BEN

(*Still taken aback.*) We'll need a license.

JACK

(*Springing up and into action.*) We'll get one today. "I take thee, Ben…"

BEN

(*Following.*) We need rings, someone to officiate, a reception…

JACK

I bet Francine would whip us up some Boston cream pies…

BEN

Pete could officiate…

JACK

Pete? He's so long-winded…

> (*They've retreated upstairs with good-natured teasing, laughing and mock-bickering as they go. Meanwhile a final projection flickers on—exterior of a lovely craftsman house circa 1910, fully restored, with drought-tolerant yard and all. We hear once again from our realtor.*)

BILL DIMMELWICH (V.O.)

At Earthly Delights, we believe in housing people for more than just one lifetime. See how yesterday's craftsmen are holding up today. Visit www.earthlydelights.com. Where houses were built for your forever.

353

(Projection image crossfades into final title card: THE END.)

END OF PLAY

ACKNOWLEDGMENTS

I have spent my lifetime in gratitude. Here are some of the people I have to thank for this book:

First, Jeanne Field, who has been looking over my shoulder for over twenty years, smiling, nodding encouragement, sometimes publishing, and frequently teaching me best practices for moving my writing from desk or desktop into the larger world.

Michael Kearns, for his beautifully wrought Foreword which he took such care to research and compose.

Juno Pinder, who carefully edited each play's copy, helping to format the whole.

Dean Abatemarco for his cover designs and James Fawcett for his photo.

And of course, my own Dan McCleary for his art and partnership.

Now on to the list of people who helped birth each of these plays and move them to production:

To my producing friends, Suzi Dietz & Lenny Beer, Paula Holt, Eileen T'Kaye, Ken Werther, the late Norma Ring, the late Paul & Sonia Verdier at Stages, Leo Garcia at Highways, Bart DeLorenzo at The Evidence Room, Craig Strong & Randy Bennett at Santa Fe Stages, David Van Asselt at Rattlestick, Sandra Szeitsew at Santa Monica Playhouse, and more recently, Sandee & Gary Grossman at Skylight Theatre Company.

To the directors, Don Amendolia, David Schweizer, Jenny Sullivan, and Elizabeth Swain, each of whom helped birth a healthy baby into the world and hand it back to this parent all clean and properly swaddled, as well as the design and production teams for each show, including the stage managers and assistant directors who lent their expertise.

And finally, to the long list—much longer than the final cast lists cited on each play's production history page shows—of actors who sat down at my table or stood on a stage to read the many drafts of each play as they developed.

It's been a privilege to be an active member of a wide, often intersecting community of playmakers.

-In lifelong gratitude, T.A.

TONY ABATEMARCO, Author

Principally known for his theatre work, Tony's first collaboration as co-writer and director of the a cappella musical BRAIN HOTEL won multiple plaudits including the first *LA Weekly* "New Directions in Theatre" Award and was subsequently selected as a representative Los Angeles event for the International Olympic Arts Festival, 1984.

Next he co-authored SIR VIVAL SWEEPSTAKES for Jacques D'Amboise's National Dance Institute at the Mark Taper Forum. His first one-man play, FOUR FATHERS, won *DramaLogue* and *LA Weekly* Awards for Best Solo Writing, excerpts of which are included in Michael Kearns' "Getting Your Solo Act Together" published by Heinemann.

IN SAMBA ZONES (later, THE NEXT BIG THING) was produced in the first Mark Taper Forum New Works Festival '88, and developed further by the Audrey SkirballKenis Foundation in '91. He was commissioned by John Densmore of The Doors to collaborate on a screenplay adaptation of Mr. Densmore's *New York Times* bestselling memoir, "Riders on the Storm."

His twelve plays to date (including the four produced ones published here) have intermittently been through development processes at LA TheatreWorks, Stages Theatre Center, LA Theatre Center, Santa Fe Stages, and at his own Skylight Theatre Company where he has served as Co-Artistic Director since 2012.

His short stories have been published in the literary magazines *Noir Mechanics*, *Boneshaker*, *High Performance*, and by Windfall Press (COLOGNE), and his songs have been covered by Suzy Andrews on her debut album "Profile" produced by Ulyseé Musique, Paris. His essays and articles have appeared in *The Los Angeles Times*, the *A.S.K.* journal, "Parabasis," lastagetimes.com, *The Santa Monica Emeritus College Journal,* the Santa Fe Playhouse's "Callboard," and in several art galleries including his husband, Dan McCleary's catalogue for his Federal Arts Project mural "American Jury" installed at the Federal Courthouse of Las Cruces, N.M.

He is a frequent reader of original material at spoken word events at Beyond Baroque, Rant&Rave at Rogue Machine, BackStory at the Victory Theatre, Spoken Interludes, Tasty Words, Highways and on both KCRW & KPFK Public Radio stations. Watch for Volume II of his as-yet-unproduced collected plays in the near future.

IMAGE: DAN MCCLEARY

www.ingramcontent.com/pod-product-compliance
Lightning Source LLC
Chambersburg PA
CBHW050028030726
47506CB00001B/168